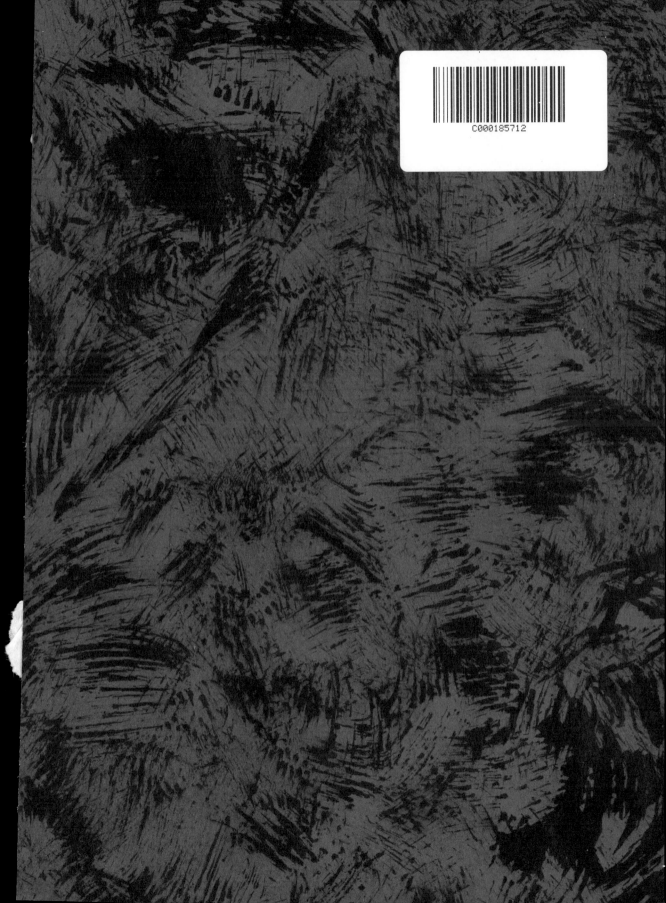

C000185712

TACO TALES

Recipes and Stories from Mexico

GINGKO PRESS

Cochinita Pibil
PP. 123–124

Pastel de Elote
PP. 142 – 143

9

Agua Fresca de Mango
P. 31

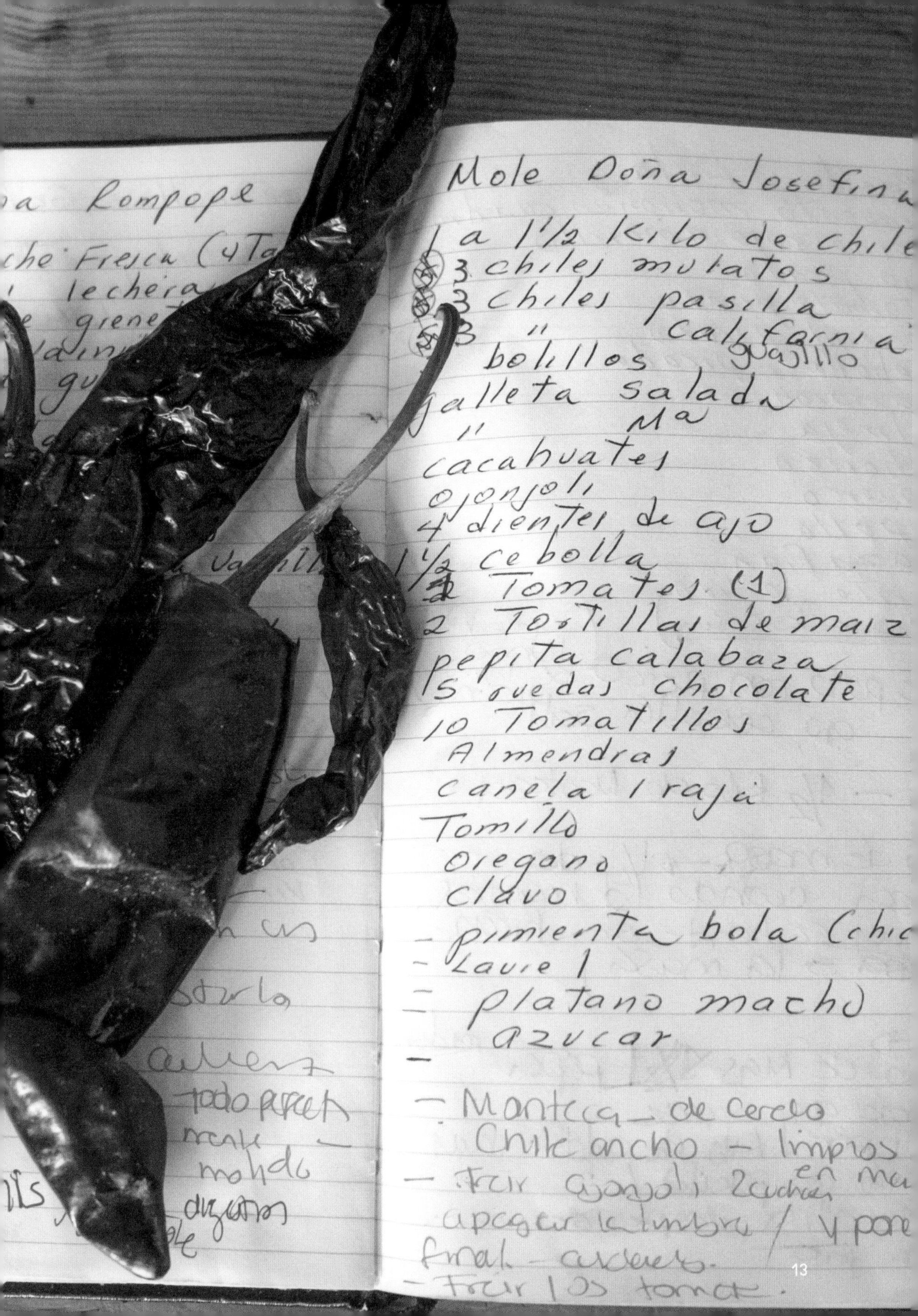

Rompope

che Fresca (1 Ta...
lecheria
grene...
di...
gu...

Vaini...

Mole Doña Josefina

1 a 1½ Kilo de chile
3 chiles mulatos
3 chiles pasilla
3 " California guajillo
bolillos
galleta salada
" Ma
cacahuates
ajonjoli
4 dientes de ajo
1½ cebolla
2 Tomates (1)
2 Tortillas de maiz
pepita calabaza
5 ovedas chocolate
10 Tomatillos
Almendras
canela 1 raja
Tomillo
Oregano
clavo
- pimienta bola (chic
- Laurel
- platano macho
- azucar
-
- Manteca de cerdo
Chile ancho - limpios
- Freir ajonjoli 2 cuchar en ma
apagar la lumbre / y po...
final - acacuel.
- Freirlos tomat.

14

PROLOGUE

This book is my personal tribute to the recipes of my family, to Mexico, our roots, our traditions and our culture. They have always been a safe ground in my life and have brought me moments of joy. They have survived time and have adapted to changes.

This recipe compilation has been possible thanks to my parents Delia and Roberto and my aunt Martha's passion to encourage their children to preserve the Mexican tradition of cooking together as a family and to understand where we come from.

I hope these recipes and traditions can find their way to the treasure box of my beloved niece and nephews, Sebastian, Ignacio, Santiago, Emilio, Nael, Valentina, Andre,

Oskar, Wim and to yours, my dear Paula, I know you have already a piece of Mexico in your heart.

I adapted these recipes to my life outside Mexico, always trying my best to maintain their originality.

My hope is that after reading this book you will get a glimpse of our ancestral traditions and feel closer to my lovely Mexico.

Ivette Pérez de Wenkel

To Willem and Oskar

Anne Wenkel

INDEX

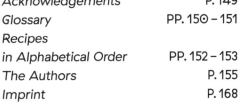

TIJUANA

BAJA CALIFORNIA

SONORA

GOLFO DE CALIFORNIA

SINALOA

DURANGO

SIERRA MADRE OCC

MEXICO

CHICHEN ITZA

GOLFO DE MEXICO

YUCATAN

CIUDAD DE MEXICO

CHIAPAS

OAXACA

TEZQUITL
Y
LIMÓN

"SUEÑOS DE LIMÓN Y MIEL"

LEMON DREAMS

Learning to cook in my mother's kitchen was not an easy task, as she is one of the fastest cooks I have ever seen, she can create delicious Enchiladas de Mole in just 15 minutes. It's fascinating to watch her and, like many other longtime cooks, she cooks with a pinch of this and a dash of that, so you can imagine how hard it is to get proper proportions and instructions out of her personal recipe notebooks. They mainly only list the name and ingredients of the given recipe, and for everything else, you have to use your skills and imagination.

Friends, family and guests have always praised my mother's cooking talents. I still remember the day I asked her how she had learned to cook.

"Before I met your father, I had no interest in cooking, I was always avoiding the kitchen and I could hardly boil an egg ... I guess I was willing to try to cook, so I started asking around, but basically I just began doing it".
Her answer gave me comfort, a sense of happiness. She made me believe that there was always a possibility to learn something, even if it seemed hard or out of my league.

I have fond memories of my father cooking for us at the weekends, of course always surrounded by one or more assistants (normally including my sister, myself and whoever else was around). My mother still makes fun of it, in the end it was never clear who was actually doing the cooking. Ever since I can remember, my parents have had a funny quirk when going to a restaurant, they try to guess the ingredients of a dish, with the aim of recreating the recipe later at home. My father always tries, without success, to persuade the waiter to spill the beans on how to make the dish. By this time, my mother is always trying to hide under the table. I should say I take great pleasure in witnessing moments like that.

I was around 9 years old when I started helping my mom in the kitchen, cutting and squeezing limes, the small green ones we have in Mexico, we call them "limon verde or limon mexicano", known in the rest of the world as key limes. Although they are called Mexican limes, they originated from Southeast Asia. The short story is that the Arabs took them to Spain, and as part of our shared history, they ended up in Mexico. Today, Mexico is one of the most important world producers of this variety. (*Botanical name is Mexican lemon / Citrus aurantifolia, S.*)

Limes are an indispensable component in the life of a Mexican, at home they were always bought by the kilos. I remember always fighting to get them to all fit inside the refrigerator.

We use them for everything, *"aguas frescas"*, guacamole, soups, sauces and sweets. When we were kids, my mother even used them as a replacement for hairspray, trying to control my sister's and my crazy curly hair, especially when she wanted to do a ponytail (our nightmare).

As a child, squeezing limes was kind of exciting, especially because I had to learn how to use a very cool tool called the *"exprimidor de limones"* (lemon squeezer), there is one in every Mexican kitchen. But the greatest challenge was learning how to choose the right limes, because Mexican limes can be bitter if they are too mature or they have brownish spots, so you always need to go for the ones that are consistently green, otherwise you will be responsible not only for making the food bitter, but also the mood of your family.

MY TIP
If you are not sure, don't squeeze the limes directly into the food; use a cup or glass instead.

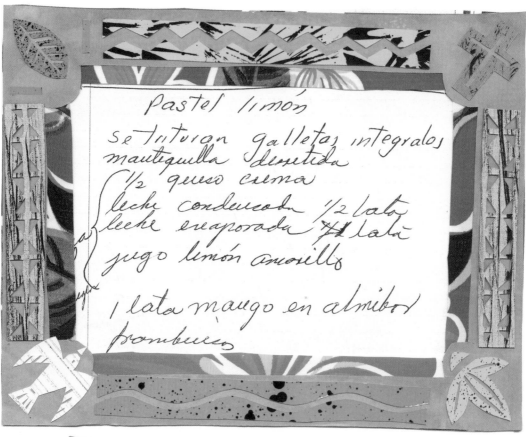

Pastel limón

se trituran galletas integrales
mantequilla derretida
½ queso crema
leche condensada ½ lata
leche evaporada ¾ lata
jugo limón amarillo

1 lata mango en almíbar
frambuesas

PAY DE LIMON — TIA AGUEDA

LEMON PIE

approx. 45 m

Crust
200g   **wholemeal crackers**
           (e.g. Honey Graham Crackers, Digestive biscuits)
90g   **melted butter**

Pie Filling
390 g   **sweetened condensed milk**
½ cup   **lemon juice**
5   **egg yolks**

Meringue to decorate
6   **egg whites**
1 ¾   **powdered sugar (icing sugar)**
1 tsp   **lemon zest**

PREPARATION

Preheat the oven to 180 ° C (350 F)

Crush the crackers into a powder. Then, by hand, mix the cracker powder with the melted butter, place it in a pie baking pan (9" or 24 cm)
and press down with the palm of your hand, covering the base and
sides. Bake the crust for about 8 minutes and remove from the oven.

For the filling: In a bowl, whisk the condensed milk and egg yolks until
blended. Then add the lemon juice and mix.

Strain the filling into a bowl and then evenly distribute on the baked
crust.
Bake for about 15–20 minutes at 180°C (350 F). When done, let the
pie cool down before adding the meringue.

For the meringue, whisk the egg whites and gradually add the
powdered sugar. Afterwards, add the lemon zest and keep mixing
all together.

Decorate with the meringue and bake briefly until golden brown.

MY TIP
Be aware that the oven
must still be very hot to
bake the meringue.

Figure
P. 24

" ... CHIA, HORCHATA, LIMON, PIÑA O TAMARINDO, QUE TOMA USTED MI ALMA?"*

*"...CHIA, RICE WATER, LEMON, PINEAPPLE OR TAMARIND, WHAT WOULD YOU LIKE TO DRINK, MY DARLING?"**

AGUA DE LA VIDA

"Aguas frescas" are traditional Mexican cold drinks, a mix of water, fruits and a sweetener (sugar, agave syrup, honey). They are the perfect pairing to enjoy a hot and spicy Mexican dish.
It is said that the tradition of drinking "aguas frescas" in Mexico comes from the 16th century and has religious origins. During the hot days of Lent (Cuaresma), Catholics used to visit and worship the Altar of the Virgin María Dolorosa, which often was placed in private homes. At the end of their prayers and before they left the house, the host would comfort them with a glass of water to continue their journey. The most popular flavours were lemon and chia, hibiscus or horchata (rice water). Some homes and churches have kept up that tradition to this today.

*Poniatowska, Elena. *Luz y luna, las lunitas.* Ediciones Era, 2007: p. 11.

Referenced from: Cedillo Vargas, Reina A., "El altar de Dolores rescate arqueológico de una tradición mexicana", *Arqueología Mexicana*, Vol. XV, No. 90 (2008).

AGUA FRESCA DE PEPINO

CUCUMBER WATER WITH LEMON AND CHIA SEEDS

approx. 10 m

1 ½ L	water
5–8 tbsp	brown sugar (agave syrup / honey)
1 handful	mint leaves
1 tbsp	chia seeds
	lime / lemon juice (4 key limes or 2 yellow lemons)
1	cucumber, unpeeled, washed

PREPARATION

Thoroughly rinse the cucumber (you can also peeled it), cut it in big pieces and put them in a blender along with the lime / lemon juice, mint leaves, sugar and chia seeds.

Serve cold, always better with ice.

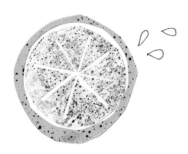

Figure
PP. 28 – 29

AGUA FRESCA DE JAMAICA

HIBISCUS WATER

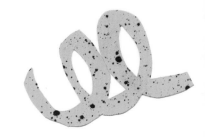

approx. 40 m

1 ½ L	water
1 cup	dried hibiscus flowers
5–8 tbsp	brown sugar (or agave syrup / honey)
1 cup	strawberries (thinly sliced)

PREPARATION

Bring 1 litre of water to a boil. Turn off the flame and add the hibiscus flowers, cover and set it aside for approx. 30 minutes.
Place a strainer on top of your glass jar, pour the concentrate through the strainer to contain the flowers. Add the rest of the water, sugar or sweetener of your preference and the ice. Sometimes it depends on the quality of the flowers to see how concentrated it is, if you find that the flavour is still too strong, you can add more water until you find your perfect taste. To serve, add the strawberry slices.

MY TIP
Don't throw away the cooked hibiscus flowers, use them as a filling for a Corn Tortilla Taco, I promise you it's delicious! With your fingers, squeeze out the remaining water. In a pan with a small amount of oil and diced onion, add the flowers, jalapeño chilli slices and season with salt and pepper. You can add avocado or any salsa for a perfect vegan taco!

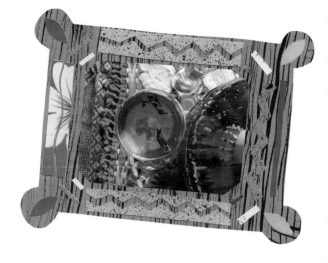

Figure
P. 8

AGUA FRESCA DE MANGO

MANGO WATER

approx. 15 m

1 ½ L	water
1–2	mangoes (depending on the size)
4	mint leaves
5–8 tbsp	brown sugar (or agave syrup / honey)

PREPARATION

Halve the mango(es) and cut out the seed. Using a spoon, scrape out the flesh of the fruit. Pour ½ litre of water and the rest of the ingredients in to a blender. Pour the concentrate into your glass jar and add the rest of the water. Add more sugar, sweetening to taste as needed. Afterwards, add the ice.

Figure
P. 12

"TU ERES MI AMOR, MI VIDA Y MI TESORO"

"YOU ARE MY LOVE, MY LIFE, MY TREASURE"

AVOCADO LOVE

I believe my mother is responsible for my devotion to avocados. When I was a baby, sitting in my kitchen chair (always hungry), crying out loud from hunger, waiting to be fed, she would give me a piece of avocado to calm me down and buy more time to finish the meal.
I have always loved everything about avocados, from the creamy texture to the smell, and of course the taste. We always have avocados in our fruit basket. It's my go-to ingredient, and I add it to almost everything: sandwiches, quesadillas, soups, tacos, salads, as a complement to meat or rice, etc.

The word avocado comes from Nahuatl (Aztec language): "ahuacatl", meaning testicle.

The Aztecs were well informed about the benefits and good nutritional properties of the avocado, they used it not only as good source of nutriment, but also in healing treatments, using the seed to make an oil they believed helped with hair and scalp problems.
The avocado is rich in vitamins A, B, C and E, and a source of minerals like calcium and potassium, and it has 15% mono-unsaturated fat, "good fat".

From this delicious fruit, Mexico has shared with the world one of my all-time favourites ... guacamole.
Guacamole is the perfect excuse to sit around the table and just enjoy.

I have been living in Europe for more than 10 years, far away from Mexico, family and friends, and I am sure it sounds strange, but guacamole has given me a sense of courage, strength, and pride. No matter where I am, there is always a friendly face when I arrive with a bowl of guacamole and tortilla chips, I can literally say guacamole has opened doors for me.

There are different recipes for guacamole, they vary from family to family. But one thing you can be sure of is that you will always find it at a barbecue, our traditional "carne asada" gatherings. Here I share with you my personal recipe and some tips that I learned during the process that will make it easier for you.

feeling home with guacamole

" ... TORTILLAS TIBIAS CON GUACAMOLE, QUE FIESTA, QUE ALEGRIA, LA MÀS CALIENTITA, LA MÀS CARIÑOSA..."*

"...WARM TORTILLAS WITH GUACAMOLE, WHAT A FIESTA, WHAT A JOY, THE WARMEST, THE MOST LOVING..."*

GUACAMOLE – THE SECRETS

The key to good guacamole is knowing how to choose a good avocado, it shouldn't feel hard or too soft, somewhere in the middle. I always like to touch the top of the avocado, if it is too soft, then leave it. I think nowadays it's easier to find good quality avocados from Mexico.

If you have a couple of days to prepare your dinner or gathering, you can buy hard avocados, cover them with old newspaper or recycled paper, and keep them inside your oven or in your kitchen cabinet. Depending on how hard they are, they may take between 2 to 4 days to mature. (Keep checking on them, it's important not to forget them, which has happen to me).

If your guests or kids do not like the raw onion flavour or the cilantro, you can marinate these ingredients with natural lemon or lime juice 20 minutes prior to preparation, that will soften the onion and cilantro and the flavour will be milder.

Molcahete (mortar): It's the traditional tool used to make and serve the guacamole, but a good bowl always works as well.

To keep the ingredients fresh, try not to prepare the guacamole more than 30 minutes before serving.

Don't add all the lemon juice at once, you need to find the perfect amount of it for your taste buds.
There's a belief that keeping the seed of the avocado in the guacamole will prevent it from turning brown; that is not true, the only thing that prevents this is lemon juice.
You can also add a half or one teaspoon of olive oil to make it creamier.

*Carlos Fuentes, *Cristóbal Nonato*, p. 408 (1987)

AVOCADO SMOOTHIE

AVOCADO SMOOTHIE

approx. 10 m

Serves 2

1	**banana (peeled and frozen)**
1	**green apple**
½	**avocado**
1 tsp	**chia seeds**
1 ½ cups	**spinach leaves**
2 cups	**milk or almond milk**

MY TIP
Put the banana in
the freezer one day in
advance.

Figure
PP. 38 – 39

PREPARATION

Add all the ingredients in a blender
and mix perfectly.
You can add more milk depending
on how thick you like your smoothie.

GUACAMOLE

CREAMY SAUCE MADE FROM PURÉED AVOCADOS

approx. 10 m

Serves 4

3–4	**avocados**
1	**large tomato (seedless and finely chopped)**
1 handful	**fresh cilantro (finely chopped)**
½	**onion (finely chopped)**
½ tbsp	**lemon or lime juice (key limes are more acidic)**
½	**jalapeño chilli (remove stem, seeds and ribs)**
1 pinch	**dry oregano**
1 tsp	**sea salt**
	pepper
1 tsp	**olive oil (optional)**

PREPARATION

Cut the avocados in half, take out the seed and with a spoon, take out
the flesh and place it into a bowl. Use a fork to mash the avocados
until you find the texture you like, I always leave some small chunks.
Add the onion, cilantro, oregano, lemon juice, salt, pepper and jalapeño chilli, mix it with a fork, add the tomato, mix and taste. Add
additional salt or lemon juice if need it, you could also add olive oil.

ROLLO DE AGUACATE
AVOCADO DIP

 approx. 50 m

1	avocado
235 g	cream cheese (room temperature)
1 handful	cilantro (finely chopped)
½	onion (finely chopped)
1	jalapeño chilli (seedless / if you can't find it fresh you can also use the marinated ones)
1	tomato (seedless and finely chopped)
½–1 tsp	salt, pepper
1 pinch	oregano
1 bag	salted tortilla chips

MY TIP
You can also make your own tortilla chips, see pages 46 – 47.

PREPARATION

Place the cream cheese into a bowl, add salt and pepper and mix it with a fork, taste it and add more salt if needed.
Add the onion, cilantro, oregano and jalapeño, mix again. Cut the avocado in half, take out the seed and, using a kitchen knife, cut the avocado into small cubes. With a spoon take out the avocado cubes and add them to the mix of cream cheese and carefully mix together. You can leave it as a normal dip, just serve it in a bowl. To make it into a roll, take a piece of aluminium foil and place it over a plate, spoon the prepared mix into the middle and fold it like a roll. Set aside in the refrigerator for 45 minutes.

TO SERVE

Take it out of the aluminium foil and place it in the middle of the serving plate. Add tortilla chips or sliced baguette around the plate.

SOPA FRIA DE AGUACATE

COLD AVOCADO SOUP

approx. 20 m

Serves 4

750 ml	**chicken broth**
2	**avocados**
½ tsp	**lime (lemon) zest**
1–2 tbsp	**lime (lemon) juice**
1 tbsp	**cilantro (finely chopped)**
1 cup	**yoghurt**
½	**jalapeño seedless (optional)**
	salt and pepper

PREPARATION

Halve the avocados, remove the seed, spoon out the flesh and place it into a bowl, add half of the lime (lemon) juice and mash it with a fork. Pour in the lime (lemon) zest and mix all together. Blend the mix together with the chicken broth, yoghurt (add more if needed), salt and pepper. Taste it and add more salt or lime (lemon) juice if needed. Place in the fridge and let it cool. When serving, you can top it off with small jalapeño slices, giving it a great spicy twist.

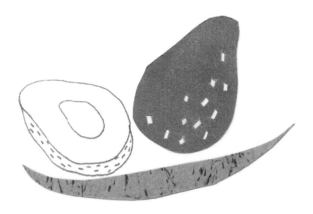

EL

MAIZ

43

"MAIZ DE MI CORAZON, QUE LLENAS MI VIDA DE ALEGRIA"*

"MY DEAREST CORN, YOU FILL MY HEART WITH JOY"*

MAGIC CORN

Corn, beans, amaranth and chia where among the most important sources of nutrition for Mayas and Aztecs.

They regarded nature as sacred, they respected and protected it. Nature was a living being, larger and more powerful than man, and they were very careful not to abuse it.

Corn always has had a very important place in Mayan traditions and festivities, they believed that man was created from corn, and many of their ceremonies are related to the growth cycle of the corn plant.

"Human flesh was made of white (male) and yellow (female) corn. Their arms and legs were made of cornmeal. The gods ground enough corn to make enough gruel to fill nine gourds, which gave men muscles, strength and power … ."
Montejo, Victor. *Popol Vuh: A Sacred book of the Mayas.* (1999)

They developed advanced techniques to grow and use the corn as part of their diet. One of their most important contributions is "nixtamalisation", the process of fermenting corn with an alkaline solution that yields corn meal to make our famous tortillas and tamales. Corn tortillas are still one of the most important components of our diet.

My first memory of shopping alone was going to the tortillería (tortilla shop). One might say that tortillerías are to Mexicans as bakeries are

to Europeans, no matter where you go, there is always one around the corner!

My mother used to pick us up every day from our primary school. After a long day at school, we were always starving. Lovely and caring as she is, she always passed by a tortillería before arriving at our school. It was always the same, 1 kg of fresh, warm tortillas gently wrapped on a pale grey paper. I can still smell them even today, there's nothing like freshly made tortillas. She always had a salt shaker in the car, and in no time she would prepare us "taquitos de sal", which we devoured in the car on our way home. Wonderful!

Handmade tortillas are still a very important source of income for many Mexican women. They sell their tortillas on the street markets or at different corners in the city. With this ancestral tradition and economic activity, many of them support their families. If you ever see a lady selling her tortillas, don't miss the opportunity to try them, they are unique and one of the most rewarding experiences, there are not many places where you will find them handmade.

In the north of Mexico, where I grew up, wheat flour tortillas "tortillas de harina", are more popular than corn tortillas. More about this later.

*Fragment of a Mayan children's poem, Waldemar Hernández (2009)

TORTILLA DE MAIZ

CORN TORTILLA

approx. 40 m

6 tortillas

1 cup	**corn flour (Mexican nixtamailised corn)**
¾ – 1 cup	**warm water**
1 pinch	**salt**

TORTILLA
is thin and flat, similar
to a crepe, made of
nixtamalised corn or
wheat flour.

Have your tortilla press ready. You need to have two sheets of cling film, it can be from a bag or any plastic. Lay one of them at the bottom of the tortilla press and the other you will use it for the top, this will prevent the dough from sticking in the press. (When you finish all your tortillas, you need to just properly clean the plastic, and you can reuse it as much as you want for future tortillas).

Put the flour in a large bowl, add the salt and mix with your hands, then pour half of the water while you keep mixing it. Gradually add more water until you your dough (masa) feels soft and not sticky. The dough should not be too dry.
Knead the dough properly for 5 minutes, then cover with a damp kitchen towel and let it rest for at least 15 minutes.
Make walnut size dough balls. If you find them too big for your tortilla press then you can make them smaller, or if needed, you can make them bigger.

Preheat your "comal" (traditional Mexican pan) or a non-stick pan (it is very important that the pan be hot).
Carefully place the dough in the pan and bake the first side of the tortilla for just a few seconds, long enough for the tortilla to be ready to turn over. Turn over the tortilla and bake the second side a little bit longer, then turn the tortilla over again and keep baking. (This process take seconds). To know when your tortillas are ready, they should inflate, you can help this process if in the last turn over, you press it gently with a kitchen towel.

MY TIP
When preparing your own tortillas, you can freeze any tortillas that you cannot eat on the same day, e.g. in packages of 5 tortillas in plastic bags in the freezer.

There are very good options for ready-made corn tortillas in Mexican or Latin shops, but I can tell you, nothing can compare to the ones you prepare by hand. Like many things in the kitchen, it requires patience and practice, but by following the instructions of this recipe, I am pretty sure you will be able to make them.

When you are preparing a recipe that requires fried tortillas, e.g. chilaquiles, flautas, tacos dorados, there is no need to make them by hand, as for this kind of recipe, it is easier to buy them ready-made.

ENCHILADAS DE MOLE
ENCHILADAS WITH MOLE SAUCE

approx. 1,5 h

Serves 6

18	corn tortillas
3	chicken breasts (cooked and shredded; keep broth)
1	large onion
1	carrot
1	garlic clove (peeled)
1 handful	parsley (finely chopped)
	oil to fry
	salt

Mole Sauce

1	jar Mole paste (eg. Doña Maria / La Costeña) you can also make your own mole (page 116)
4–5 cups	chicken broth
1	garlic clove
¼	onion
100 g	Mexican chocolate (eg. Abuelita / Ibarra) or using any dark chocolate with at least 55% cacao.
10	unsalted peanuts
10	almonds
2	tomatoes
1 tbsp	sesame seeds
1 tbsp	sugar

To Serve

50g	Feta, Pecorino or Mexican "Cotija" cheese.
200g	sour cream
1	onion (white or red) finely chopped and marinated with 3 tbsp of apple vinegar (marinate for a minimum of 30 minutes).

ENCHILADA
is a corn tortilla, rolled,
filled and covered in sauce.
There are many ways of
preparing them, depending
on the region. The most
popular filling is chicken,
but there are some
vegetarian varieties too.

PREPARATION

In a large pot, cook the chicken along with 1½ litres of water, half an onion, carrot and garlic. Bring it to a boil, then reduce the flame, cover it, and keep cooking until it's done. Take out the chicken and shred it, (keep the broth). With a little bit of oil, sauté the chicken together with the chopped onion and parsley, reserve.

Blend together 1 cup of chicken broth, and all the ingredients of the mole sauce except for the chocolate.

In a deep pot, heat a little bit of oil and pour the mole mixture, add another 2 cups of chicken broth, bring to a boil and then reduce the heat, stirring continuously. The mole sauce should be creamy but not too thick. Add the chocolate and keep stirring until it melts, taste, and add salt if need it. If it's too spicy, you can add more chocolate or sugar, and if you find it too thick, add more chicken broth.

MY TIP
When you are using store bought tortillas, they can be a little bit dry. To make them softer, sprinkle a few drops of water before you heat them.

TO SERVE

Heat your tortillas on both sides until soft, place them in individual serving plates, (I normally serve 3 enchiladas per person). Fill them with chicken, roll them and pour the mole sauce over the rolled tortillas, enough to cover them.

Top them off with a spoonful of sour cream, cheese and marinated onions. You can serve the enchiladas with a portion of refried beans (p. 146), guacamole and rice.

Traditionally in Mexico, tortillas are previously fried, but in my family we love this lighter version.

Figure
PP. 50–51

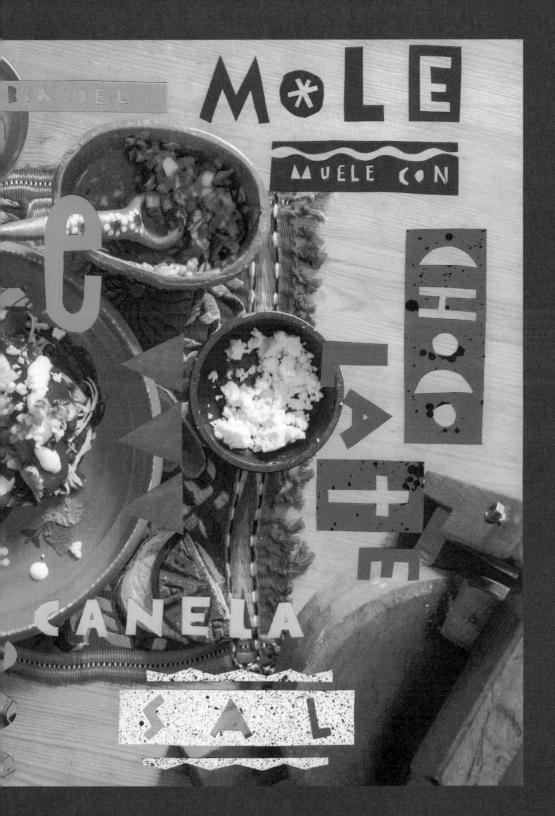

ENCHILADAS VERDES CON CREMA

CREAMY TOMATILLO SAUCE ENCHILADAS

approx. 1,5–2 h

Serves 6

18	corn tortillas (pages 46–47)
3	chicken breasts (cooked and shredded; keep broth)
3	garlic cloves (peeled)
½	onion
1	bay leaf
1	carrot (peeled)
1	leek
1	stalk of celery
1 pinch	oregano
	salt
	pepper

for the sauce

10–12	green tomatillos
½ cup	chicken broth
½	jalapeño chilli (seedless)
½	onion
1	garlic clove
3 handfuls	fresh cilantro
200 g	sour cream or crème fraîche
	salt and pepper
100 g	grated cheese (Monterey Jack, Mozzarella, Gouda)

You can also buy an ready–made salsa verde.

MY TIP
Instead of chicken breast you can also cook half a chicken. This will add more flavour to the chicken broth.

If you are using an already made salsa verde you only need to add ¼ cup of chicken broth, fresh cilantro, sour cream and a little salt to the sauce. Store–bought salsa verde are usually spicy.

PREPARATION

In a big pot with water, cook the chicken together with the leek, garlic, onion, bay leaf, carrot, celery, salt and pepper, bring to a boil, reduce the heat and cover it. When it's ready, keep the broth and shred the chicken, set aside.

FOR THE TOMATILLO SAUCE

In a medium pot with boiling water, pour in the tomatillos, onion, jalapeño and garlic, reduce the heat and cook until the tomatillos change colour (the tomatillos should not be too soft). Remove all the ingredients (drain the water) and mix them in a blender along with the sour cream, cilantro, oregano, salt and pepper and 1 ½ cups of chicken broth. Season and add salt and jalapeño if necessary.

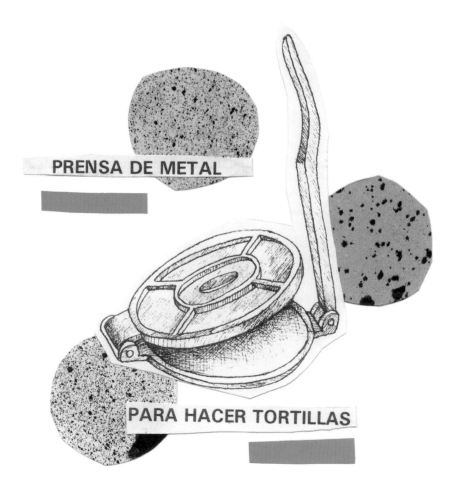

PRENSA DE METAL

PARA HACER TORTILLAS

Preheat the oven to 180°C (350 F). In a pot with a little bit of oil, heat the sauce, stirring occasionally (about 15 minutes).

Heat the corn tortillas on both sides until softened. Fill them with chicken, and roll them up. Place them side-by-side in a casserole dish. Pour the sauce evenly over the rolled tortillas and sprinkle with the grated cheese.

Bake the enchiladas at 180°C (350 F) for about 10 to 15 minutes until the cheese has completely melted.

TO SERVE

Figure
P. 7

These enchiladas are usually served with rice, refried beans or guacamole (page 37).

POZOLE VERDE CON POLLO

GREEN HOMINY AND CHICKEN STEW

approx. 1 h

Serves 4

6 cups	hominy for pozole, cooked or canned (the liquid is also used)
½	chicken
½	onion
3	garlic cloves (peeled)
1	bay leaf
1 ½ L	water

For the sauce

8–10	fresh Tomatillos halved (if not available fresh, you can replace them with canned tomatillos)
100 g	pumpkin seeds
½	jalapeño chilli (seedless)
2 handfuls	fresh cilantro
1	poblano chilli (roasted and cut into strips) (you can also replace it with a can of poblano chillies 220 g)
½	onion
½ tsp	cumin
3	garlic cloves (peeled)
1 handful	radish leaf
1 tsp	oregano
1 tsp	dried or fresh epazote (optional)
	salt
	pepper

MY TIP
You can find the spice "Epazote" in Latin American Super Markets or order it online.

To Serve

4	radishes cut into thin slices
1	iceberg lettuce cut into thin strips
1	avocado (sliced)
	lime or lemon juice
	oregano depending on your taste

PREPARATION

In a large pot, cook the chicken with the water, onion, garlic cloves, salt and bay leaf. After cooking, remove the chicken and shred it. Drain the broth and set aside.

FOR THE SAUCE

First roast the pumpkin seeds in a pan without oil and set aside (don't let them burn).
Then fry the onion and garlic cloves with a little bit of oil. Add the jalapeño and poblano chillies, sauté briefly and finally add the tomatillos, pumpkin seeds and at the very end add the cilantro, radish leaves and sauté briefly.
Put everything in a blender and mix together with cumin, oregano and some chicken broth, enough for the ingredients to mix smoothly.

Fry the green sauce with a little bit of oil on a pan, season with salt and pepper, taste and add more salt if necessary.

Heat the rest of the chicken broth in a large saucepan. Add the chicken, green sauce and the white pozole corn along with its own juice. Cook for 10 minutes.

TO SERVE

Pour a portion of pozole into soup bowls, garnish with radish slices, iceberg lettuce and avocado, if you like, you can also add some drops of lime or lemon juice and a dash of oregano.

POZOLE
The name comes from the Nahuatl "pozolli" and means "foam". It is a pre-Hispanic stew, based on nixtamalised corn kernels. This specialty is one of our favourite dishes, especially on holidays like Christmas or Mexican Independence Day. Depending on the region, the pozole may be green, red or white.

Figure
PP. 56 – 57

CHILAQUILES ROJOS AL HORNO
FRIED CORN TORTILLA CHIPS COVERED WITH SALSA ROJA

approx. 30 m

The chipotle chilli is spicy, you can alternatively use 1 teaspoon of the adobo juice.

Serves 4

10	corn tortillas for the totopos (tortilla chips)
120 g	sour cream or crème fraîche
60 g	grated Monterey Jack, Gouda, Mozzarella or Pecorino cheese
4	tomatoes
1	garlic clove (peeled)
½	onion
½ tsp	oregano
½	chipotle chilli in adobo (canned "chipotle")
	salt and pepper
1 handful	fresh cilantro
	oil for frying

CHILAQUILES
are triangular or rectangular cut corn tortillas, deep fried in oil, traditionally called totopos (tortilla chips) and covered with a spicy sauce, this can be any green, red or mole sauce.

A delicious breakfast! After a long party, something salty and spicy is always welcomed. In Mexico, we like to eat our chilaquiles especially at weekends. For this recipe, it is better to use already made corn tortillas or homemade tortillas, which are a day or two old.

PREPARATION

For the totopos (tortilla chips), cut the corn tortillas into triangles like the famous tortilla chips and fry in a deep pan with hot oil for about 3 minutes. Depending on the size of the pan, do not fry too many chips at the same time, so they won't stick together. The chips should be crispy but not burnt, as otherwise they may become bitter. Place the chips on kitchen paper towels to drain the excess oil.
In a medium pot, cook the tomatoes and onion briefly with enough water to cover them. When they are ready, drain them. Peel the tomatoes and mix together with the onion, garlic, chipotle chilli, oregano, cilantro, salt and pepper. In a saucepan, fry the sauce with a little bit of oil and season with salt.

Preheat the oven to 180°C (350 F).

Lay the tortilla chips in a ceramic dish or on a baking tray, cover with the sauce and sprinkle with cheese. Bake the chilaquiles for about 10 minutes until the cheese has melted.

TO SERVE

The chilaquiles are served with refried beans (page 126), sour cream and slices of avocado.

CHILAQUILES VERDES
FRIED CORN TORTILLAS CHIPS COVERED
WITH SALSA VERDE

approx. 30 m

Serves 4

10	corn tortillas (not fresh, preferably a bit dry)
100 g	Salsa Verde (from a can / jar, e.g. "La Costeña")
60 g	grated Gouda / Mozzarella or Pecorino cheese
2 handfuls	cilantro
200 g	sour cream or crème fraîche
½ tsp	chicken stock or salt
	oil for frying

PREPARATION

For the totopos (tortilla chips), cut the corn tortillas into triangles like the famous tortilla chips and fry in a deep pan with hot oil for about 3 minutes. Depending on the size of the pan, do not fry too many chips at the same time, so they won't stick together. The chips should be crispy but not burnt, as otherwise they may become bitter. Place the chips on kitchen paper towels to drain the excess oil.

In a blender, mix the Salsa Verde with the cilantro, sour cream and chicken stock. Fry the sauce in a saucepan with a little bit of oil (5 minutes).

Preheat the oven to 180°C (350 F).
Lay the tortilla chips in a ceramic dish or on a baking tray, cover them with the green sauce and sprinkle with cheese. Bake for about 10 minutes until the cheese has melted.

TO SERVE

The chilaquiles are served with refried beans (page 126), sour cream and slices of avocado.

I adapted this recipe during my university years, I never had the time to make my own salsa verde. Of course I recommend that you make your own salsa verde, but this recipe comes in very handy when you are hungry and don't have time. See the Salsa Verde recipe on page 56.

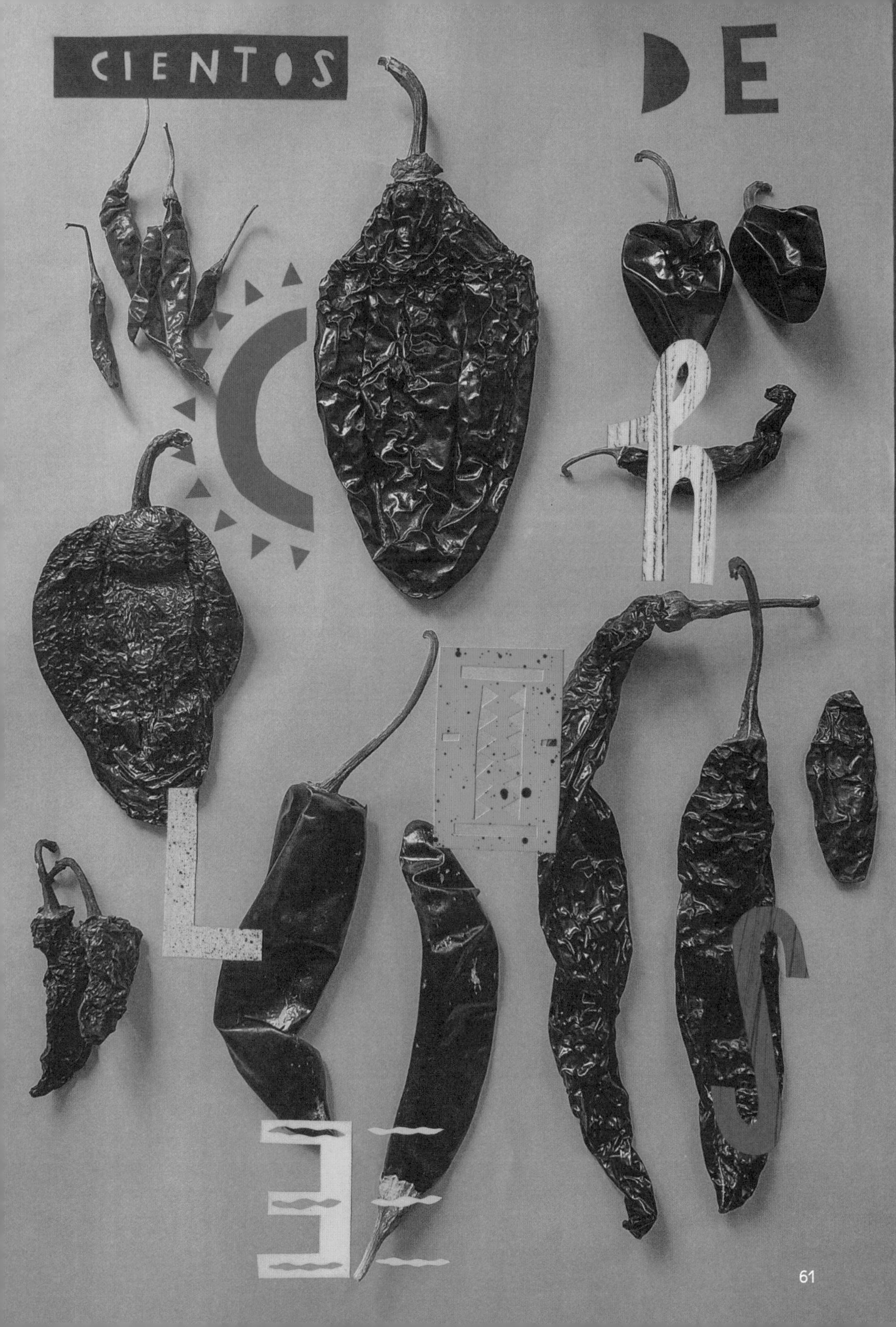
CIENTOS DE
CHILES

"YO SOY COMO EL CHILE VERDE, LLORONA, PICANTE PERO SABROSO"

"I AM LIKE A GREEN CHILLI PEPPER, LLORONA, SPICY HOT, BUT TASTY."

CHILLI & SAUCES

The name chilli comes from the Náhuatl, "chilli" or "xilli". Chilli is one of the oldest plants in Mesoamerica. The species "Capsicum annuum", has its origin in Mexico, and there are more than 60 different varieties of it. Our ancestors used them not just as part of their daily diet but also as treatment for various diseases such as tuberculosis, earache and as a painkiller.

The Spanish physician and naturalist Francisco Hernández de Toledo (1514–1587) extensively toured the new world and created a classification of the Mexican plants and their benefits. He considered chilli "bad for the soul, as it stimulates sensuality". That could be one of the reasons why Mexican hot chillies where not popular in Spain.

Chilli is our favourite spice. As Mexicans, we learn to enjoy the taste of chilli at an early age, it is a normal ingredient in many of our sweets, candies and fruit salads.
Every day in front of my elementary school there was a lovely man with a converted bicycle selling delicious mangos on a stick, jicamas or salads made from the fruit of your choice. I liked mine

with coconut, pineapple, watermelon, cucumber, oranges and jicama always seasoned with a mix of lime juice, salt and chilli powder or chilli sauce. I no longer remember the man's face, but I still remember his amazing homemade chilli sauce. In America and some countries in Europe, it is now easy to find a delicious chilli powder called *tajín*. You can add it to your favourite fruits or any salad.

In Mexico we love "enchilarnos", i.e. the enjoyable feeling we experience after eating something so spicy, your mouth, tongue and even your whole throat are burning. All your senses come to life, you can even become tearful, sweaty and begin to hyperventilate. We love that feeling and cannot get enough of it.
My mother is one of the few Mexicans that I know who does not enjoy spicy food.
The recipes for the sauces, which are presented here, are usually a milder version of the original recipes. The good thing is you can add as much chilli as you like.

You will be able to find a great variety of fresh and dried chillies outside of Mexico.

SALSA DE CHILE HABANERO CON CEBOLLA MORADA

CHILLI HABANERO AND RED ONION SAUCE

approx. 10 m

1	red onion thinly sliced
3	radishes cut into thin slices
½	habanero chilli, thinly sliced (remove stems, seeds and ribs)
	juice of 3 limes or 2 lemons.
2 tbsp	apple cider vinegar or white wine vinegar
1–2 cups	hot water (enough to cover the ingredients)
	oregano
	sea salt
	pepper

PREPARATION

Add the onion, radishes and habanero chilli in a medium bowl. Add the hot water until all ingredients are perfectly covered. Then add the lime juice, vinegar, oregano, salt and pepper to the bowl, stir and leave to marinate for at least one hour.

The habanero chilli is one of the hottest chillies in Mexico, please be careful when handling it. If you have latex gloves, use them and make sure to wash your hands several times afterwards, and do not touch your face.

Figure
P. 164

SALSA DE TOMATILLO VERDE

TOMATILLO VERDE SAUCE

approx. 10 m

8–12	tomatillos verdes (Mexican green tomatoes)
¼	onion
1	garlic clove (peeled)
½	jalapeño chilli (remove stems, seeds and ribs)
1 handful	fresh cilantro finely chopped
½ tsp	oregano
	salt and pepper

PREPARATION ~ GRILLED SALSA VERSION

In a pan without oil, grill all ingredients (except for the cilantro). In a blender, mix all the grilled ingredients together with salt, pepper and cilantro. Season to taste.

PREPARATION ~ COOKED SALSA

Boil the jalapeño chilli and tomatoes. Make sure the water covers the tomatillos completely. When the tomatillos change colour (they do not have to be too soft), take out the tomatillos and chilli, bring them to a blender and mix all together with the cilantro, onion, garlic, salt and pepper. Season to taste.

MY TIP
You can use this salsa with tacos, chilaquiles, enchiladas.

SALSA VERDE CON AGUACATE

TOMATILLO AND AVOCADO SAUCE

approx. 10 m

5–8	tomatillos verdes
¼	onion
½ – 1	avocado
1	garlic clove
1	jalapeño chilli (remove seeds and ribs)
1 handful	fresh cilantro chopped
	salt and pepper

PREPARATION

Using a pan without oil, grill all ingredients (except for the cilantro and the avocado). Then put everything in a blender and mix together with avocado, cilantro, salt and pepper. Season to taste.

Figure
P. 67

ZANAHORIAS CURTIDAS

PICKLED CARROTS

approx. 1 h

1 kg	carrots
1	large onion (cut into thin slices)
1 tsp	dried oregano
½ tbsp	sea salt
½ tsp	black peppercorns
1	bay leaf
1 cup	vinegar (apple cider vinegar or white wine vinegar)
1 ½ cups	hot water

PREPARATION

Peel the carrots and cut into thick slices. Put all the ingredients in a bowl, heat the water and cover them with hot water. Let them rest for at least one hour.

If you wish, you can also add a jalapeño chilli.

SALSA DE MANGO Y CHILE HABANERO

CHILLI HABANERO AND MANGO SAUCE

approx. 10 m

¼	habanero chilli (remove stem, seeds and ribs)
¼	red onion
1	garlic clove (peeled)
1	mango (seed removed)
	salt and pepper

PREPARATION

In a pan without oil, briefly grill the habanero chilli, the onion and garlic. In a blender, mix all the ingredients together with salt and pepper until you have a puree consistency and texture. Taste and add more salt or chilli if needed.

This exotic sauce goes very well with meat and it's my favourite for tacos al pastor.

This chilli is one of the hottest chillies in Mexico. I recommend using latex gloves when cutting it. Wash your hands well and avoid any contact to your eyes or face.

MY TIP
For this recipe, I used only a quarter habanero chilli. It's hot enough for me.

MOLCAJETE

SALSA DE CHILE DE ARBOL

CHILE DE ÁRBOL SAUCE

approx. 15 m

2	tomatoes cut in quarters
1	clove garlic (peeled)
2 to 5	dry chile de árbol (remove the stem)
1 pinch	oregano
	salt
1 tbsp	oil

MY TIP
It's better to add the chilli gradually. My grandmother always used 5 chillies for this recipe, but that is way too spicy for me.

PREPARATION

In a pan with hot oil fry all ingredients. Begin with the tomatoes, then garlic, and finally add the chillies (be careful not to burn the chillies). For my salsa, I normally use just 2 chillies. In a blender, mix all ingredients along with salt. Taste and add more salt if needed.

SALSA DE CHILE DE ARBOL ASADO

GRILLED CHILE DE ÁRBOL SAUCE

approx. 30 m

10	dry chile de árbol
1	onion chopped into small cubes
2 handfuls	fresh cilantro, finely chopped
	juice of 3 limes or 2 lemons
1 pinch	oregano
	sea salt and pepper

This is a unique recipe from my great grandmother Abuelita Carmen. Delicious but also challenging. Keep the kids out of the kitchen, the door closed and the window open. The roasting chillies create a very spicy, smoky atmosphere you'll feel in your throat. When roasting chillies, I have to go to the window to catch some fresh air. If you have an extractor fan, turn it on.

PREPARATION

Carefully and quickly grill the chillies in a hot pan without oil, making sure not to burn them!
Then cut off the stems and cut the chillies into small pieces using kitchen scissors.

Crush the chillies in a mortar or molcajete. Add the rest of the ingredients and mix everything. Depending on the taste, you can add more lime / lemon juice or salt. I always like to make it with a good amount of lime juice so it's milder. Let it rest for at least 30 minutes. This salsa will dry after some hours, you can keep adding lime / lemon juice if you like.

SALSA ROJA
RED TOMATO SAUCE

approx. 10 m

3	large tomatoes
½	onion
1 handful	fresh cilantro (chopped)
1	garlic clove (peeled)
½	jalapeño chilli (or chile de árbol)
	salt and pepper

Figure
P. 70

PREPARATION

Using a pan, grill all ingredients except the cilantro. Add them to a blender and mix all together with salt, pepper and cilantro. Season to taste.

SALSA PICO DE GALLO
FRESH CHOPPED TOMATOES AND ONION SAUCE

approx. 10 m

4	large tomatoes cut into small cubes (removed the seeds)
1	red onion cut into small cubes
½	jalapeño chilli finely chopped (stem, seeds and ribs removed)
1 handful	fresh cilantro (finely chopped)
2 tbsp	lime juice or lemon juice
1 tbsp	olive oil
1 pinch	oregano
	sea salt and pepper

PREPARATION

You just need to add all the ingredients into a bowl, mix them up and your sauce is ready.
Salsa pico de gallo goes well with salted tortilla chips and with tacos de pescado!

MY TIP
You can add fresh pineapple. Cut in small cubes, this will add an exotic and incredible taste to your sauce.

HIDALGO

ASTILLA
$15 ºº KILO.

EJOTES
$25 ºº

TUMATILLO

CHAYOTE
$3 ºº KILO.

EL MERCADO

"FIESTA A LOS SENTIDOS"

"FEAST FOR THE SENSES"

STREET MARKET AND FOOD

My parents got married when my father was finishing his training as a specialised doctor, and because of his further studies, until I was 7 years old we travelled back and forth between the fisherman's village of "El Cabezón" in the State of Sinaloa, the beautiful beaches of Izamal in Yucatan, and the mixture of exotic flavours and scents of the street market of Villa Coapa in Mexico City, where we lived at my grandparents' house, abuelita Fulvia and abuelito Javier (my father's side).

For my parents, it was a difficult time, no money, my dad would spend most of the day at university and we would hardly see him, my mother spent most of the time alone, in a big city, and for someone from the north of Mexico, this was overwhelming, like being in a foreign country. But for me, it was a dream, I remember those days with joy, always playing outside with my siblings and cousins, having fun.

I still remember the mix of exotic flavours and aromas of the Villa Coapa Street Market.
The street markets (Tianguis) in Mexico are full of pre–Hispanic traditions, one of my favourites is eating at the market. The food you will find here evokes the idea of comfort, a warm feeling, flavours and aromas from home.
The Spanish were amazed at the meticulous planning of the markets and their immense variety of products. One of the biggest markets was developed during the times of King Moctezuma, "El Mercado de Tlatelolco", the Tlatelolco Market in Tenochtitlan, the Capital of the Aztec empire, now Mexico City. ... *"When we arrived at the great market place, called Tlaltelolco, we were astounded at the number of people and the quantity of merchandise that it contained, ... we had never seen such a thing before ..."*
Diaz del Castillo, Bernardo. *The True History of the Conquest of New Spain* (2011).

During the 9 months that I lived in Mexico City, I almost never passed up an opportunity to go to these street markets. Every Sunday morning, as a ritual, we would wake up at 6am and my grandmother would prepare the colourful plastic market shopping bags, I would take her hand, and together we would embark on an incredible journey, and we witnessed the most creative ways that I have ever seen to sell a product.
Cooking was not my grandmother's strength, but she always knew where to find the best food stalls to have breakfast, we always stopped by an old lady sitting on the floor making incredible quesadillas de flor de calabaza (zucchini flower), with handmade blue corn tortillas. Quesadillas, flautas, sopes and tacos are among the vast array of food options you will find at the market. Over the years, the street markets have kept their reputation for being the perfect place to discover and enjoy easy, authentic, and affordable Mexican food. Don't hesitate to try it, you will feel at home!

77

TACOS DE POLLO AL PASTOR

TACOS WITH ADOBO MARINATED CHICKEN

Serves 4

approx. 1,50 h

500 g	chicken breast fillets
12	corn tortillas

For the adobo (Pastor) marinade

1	dried guajillo chilli
1	dried ancho chilli
1	dried chipotle chilli
1 tsp	achiote paste (Mexican spice)
2	tomatoes (seedless)
¼	onion
1	garlic clove (peeled)
½ tbsp	oregano
½ cup	pineapple in cubes (optional)
¼ cup	orange juice
1 tbsp	apple or white wine vinegar
1 tsp	salt
½ tsp	cumin

Garnish

1 cup	grilled pineapple cubes
	(On a baking sheet, add the pineapple slices and brush them with a little bit of oil. Bake in the oven for approx. 10 minutes, turning them over halfway through, and cutting them into cubes when done)

You can use the "salsa" of your choice.

1	avocado
2 handfuls	cilantro (chopped)
½	onion (finely chopped)
	Salsa de chile de árbol (page 69)
	Salsa de mango y habanero (page 68)

TACOS

Tacos are corn or wheat flour tortillas filled with your choice of meats, seafood or vegetables. Normally, in Mexico tacos are always eaten together with a spicy sauce. Tacos are a classic example of "Mexican fast food" you can find all over the city. We call these places "Taquerias". This versatile dish has pre–Hispanic origins, we have enjoyed some version of tacos since the time of the Aztecs. For many years they were considered food for the working class, but thanks to their appealing taste and the inspiration of cooks and chefs all over the world, these days tacos are considered one of the most popular and liked meals.

Tacos al Pastor are originally from Mexico City. They are an adaptation of Arab shawarma created by the influence of immigrants from Libya and Syria in the 60's.

PREPARATION

Cut the dry chillies lengthwise, remove seeds and ribs. In a saucepan, bring water to a boil, turn off the heat and add the chilli peppers until they are softened.
Grill the tomatoes, then remove the seeds. In a blender, mix the chillies, tomatoes and remaining ingredients, taste and add salt if needed. Slice the chicken breasts as thinly as you can and put them in a bowl, marinate them with the sauce, cover the bowl and let it rest in the refrigerator for at least 1 hour. Fry the marinated chicken breast fillets with a little bit of oil, then cut them into thin strips.

TO SERVE

Heat the corn tortillas on both sides and fill them with the chicken. Add some cilantro and onion, grilled pineapple, salsa and guacamole or slices of avocado.

Figures
PP. 76 – 77, 162

FLAUTAS DE POLLO
CHICKEN STUFFED FRIED ROLLED TORTILLAS

approx. 30 m

Serves 4

12	corn tortillas
3	chicken breast fillets (you can optionally fill them with mashed potatoes or shredded beef)
oil	for frying
½	large onion
1	bay leaf
	toothpicks

Garnish

	sour cream / crème fraîche
30 g	Feta or Pecorino grated cheese
1	iceberg lettuce cut into thin strips
	radishes cut into thin slices
	Guacamole (page 37)
	Salsa Roja or Salsa de Tomatillo Verde (pages 71 / 65)
	refried beans (page 126)

PREPARATION

In a pot with water, cook the chicken breast along with the onion, salt and the bay leaf. Take out the chicken and shred it.

Heat the tortillas on both sides and fill them with some of the shredded chicken (not too much). Now roll up the tortillas like a flute (flauta) and seal with a toothpick (use two if necessary). Heat 1–2 cups of oil in a pot or deep frying pan and fry the flautas until golden brown.

TO SERVE

Arrange 3 of them on each plate. Spread the iceberg lettuce, radish slices, and Salsa Roja / Salsa Tomatillo Verde on the Flautas. Add sour cream and sprinkle with cheese.
Serve the flautas warm with guacamole and refried beans on the side.

FLAUTAS
The name comes because from its similarity to the musical instrument, the flute. The main characteristic of flautas is that the corn tortillas are rolled, and stuffed with any filling and then fried in oil until crispy.

Figure
P. 81

QUESADILLAS DE CHORIZO
QUESADILLA WITH CHORIZO

approx. 15 m

Serves 4

12	**corn or wheat flour tortillas**
100 g	**mild chorizo**
200 g	**Mexican Oaxaca, Monterey Jack, Mozzarella or Gouda cheese**

Garnish

avocado cut in slices
salsa of your choice
refried beans (page 126)

PREPARATION

Cut the chorizo into small pieces and cook over medium heat without oil, when ready, set aside. On a pan or "comal", warm the tortillas on both sides, place the cheese and chorizo in the centre, fold and heat them on both sides until the cheese has melted.

TO SERVE
Open the quesadillas slightly, place 1 or 2 avocado slices, add salsa and serve them together with refried beans.

QUESADILLAS
are corn or wheat flour tortillas filled with cheese and other ingredients. Feel free to experiment. They can be fried or baked in a pan. One of my favourite childhood dinners!

COMAL DE HOJALATA

QUESADILLAS DE FLOR DE CALABAZA

QUESADILLA WITH ZUCCHINI FLOWERS

Serves 4

approx. 20 m

12	**corn tortillas**
12	**zucchini flowers (fresh or canned)**
½	**jalapeño chilli (remove stems, seeds and ribs)**
½	**onion (finely chopped)**
200 g	**Mexican Oaxaca, Monterey Jack, Mozzarella or Gouda cheese**
	salt
1	**garlic clove (peeled and finely chopped)**
	oil for frying

PREPARATION

For the filling, cut the zucchini flowers into large pieces and finely chop the jalapeño chilli.

In a pan with a little bit of oil, lightly fry the onion and garlic on low heat. Add chopped jalapeño chilli and sauté briefly. Finally, add the zucchini flowers, sauté for 5 minutes and season with salt.

Warm the tortillas lightly on both sides, place the cheese and the zucchini flower preparation in the centre of the tortillas, fold and heat them on both sides until the cheese has melted.

TO SERVE

You can eat them as they are, or you can open the quesadillas slightly, add avocado slices and the salsa of your choice. These quesadillas are one of a kind.

SOPES CON PAPA Y CHORIZO

SOPES WITH POTATO AND CHORIZO

approx. 45 m

To prepare the masa, just follow the recipe of Corn Tortillas (page 47)

You can swap the potatoes and chorizo with minced meat or shredded chicken.

Serves 4

8	Sopes
3	potatoes peeled and cut into small cubes
200 g	mild chorizo, cut in to small pieces
2 cups	refried beans (page 126)

Dough (masa) for the Sopes

400 g	cornflour (Mexican nixtamalised)
2 cups	lukewarm water
½ tsp	salt

Garnish

½	iceberg lettuce (shopped into thin strips)
4	radishes (thin slices)
30 g	Feta, Pecorino, or any Mexican grated cheese
	sour cream or crème fraîche
1	avocado (sliced)
	Salsa de Chile de Árbol (or a sauce of your choice)
	oil for frying
	salt

PREPARATION

Fry the potato cubes in a pan with oil on medium heat until they are done. Then add the chorizo, reduce heat and continue to fry everything together until the chorizo is ready. Stir regularly so that potatoes and chorizo do not burn.

Making the Sopes.
Heat (medium heat) a pan or Mexican comal. Make walnut-sized balls with the masa, place them in a bowl and cover them with a damp cloth (such as a tea towel), which will keep them moist. Press the masa balls (lightly) into a round, flat bread, you can use your hands or a tortilla press, similar to making tortillas, but sopes are smaller and thicker, about 5 mm thick.

SOPES
Deeply fried thick tortillas. They look like a small basket, and you can eat them with meat, cheese, vegetables and spicy sauces.

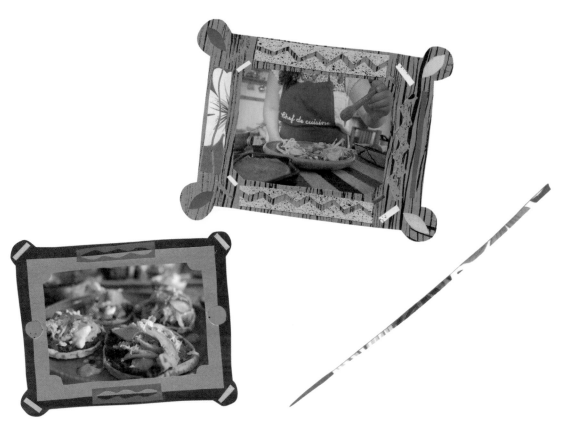

Briefly cook on a pan or comal (medium heat) on both sides, this should be fast (less than 1 minute each side). Place them on a clean surface and with the help of kitchen paper or a kitchen towel, start forming the border, pinching the edges with your fingers, like a little basket. Cover it again with the kitchen towel until you finish all the sopes.

In a pan with hot oil fry briefly the sopes on both sides until golden brown. Then place the sopes on a paper towel to drain off excess oil.

TO SERVE

To fill the sopes, first spread a tablespoon of refried beans, then add 2 tablespoons of the potato – chorizo mixture. Garnish with iceberg lettuce, radish slices, avocado, sour cream, salsa and cheese.

Figure
P. 166

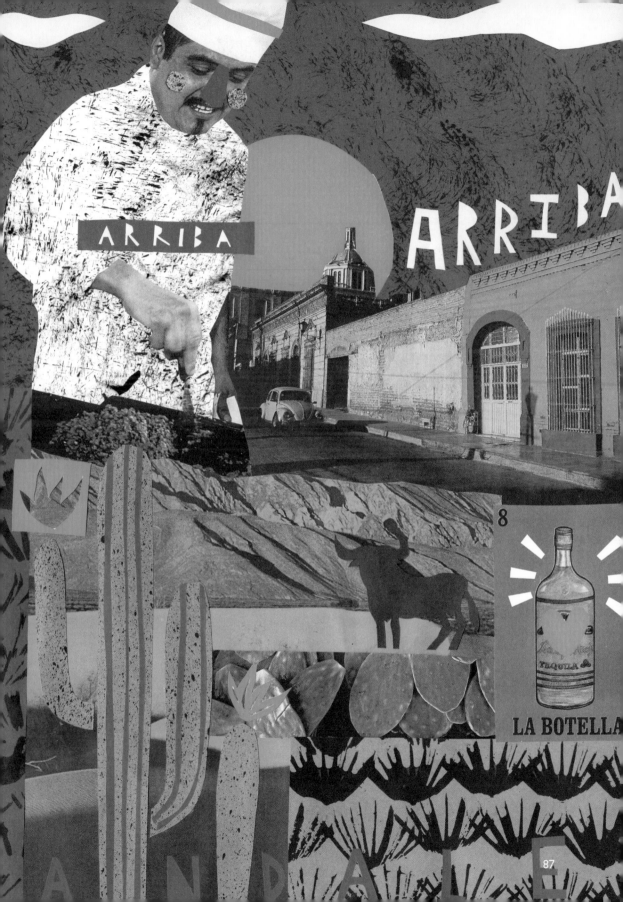

ARRIBA

ARRIBA

8

LA BOTELLA

FASCINATING NORTH – SIMPLE AND TASTY

At the time my father finished his medical studies, my family decided to move to Mexicali, Baja California, in the north of Mexico. We call this area "La Frontera" or "Franja Fronteriza" because it borders with the United States of America …"el otro lado".

En el Norte
Estados Unidos,
En el Sur Mexico,
En medio de Este
A Oeste
Una franja

In the North
the United States,
In the South, Mexico
In the middle, from east to west a
border zone

Crosthwaite, Luis Humberto. *Instrucciones para Cruzar la Frontera*, (2012), p. 161.

Here was where I recognised for the first time the smell of the fresh Tortillas de Harina, (Wheat-flour tortillas), hand-crafted by my lovely grandmother Agueda (my mother's mother). Her tortillas were unique, she worked wonders with a little bit of water, oil and flour. I could stay seated for long hours in the kitchen watching her, eating and hearing the funny stories about my mom's childhood. For many years the tortillas made of wheat flour were barely known in the south of Mexico.

It took some time until I realised that my siblings and I where living between two worlds, the one from my mother's side who was born and raised in the north (Sonora) and the one from my father's side, who was born and brought up in the south (Chiapas), in fact he was the first one in his family to travel to the north.

Mexico is a big country, and Mexicali is far away from the South, it takes you more than 3 hours to fly to Mexico City, the capital.
Certainly, the roots of our culture are in Central and South Mexico. Here is where you see, smell and touch the soul of our ancient traditions, everything is multicolour, vibrant and an explosion of art, history and incredible aromas.

My siblings and I consider ourselves norteños (people born and raised in the north). I was born in Mexico City, but Mexicali is my hometown, so I am a norteña.

100% BLUE AGAVA
TEQUILA

The weather in Mexicali is extremely hot during the summer (it can get as hot as 120°F (48°C), the hot temperatures start in May and continue until October) and compared to the south, it can be considerably cold during the winter season. People from the south have the impression that we norteños are a little bit cold and straightforward, of course the weather has always played a great role, not just in people's character, but also in their diet.

For years it was impossible to get all the exotic fruits, herbs, and vegetables that are part of the culinary tradition in Mexico. In general, we could say that the way of preparing food and dishes in the north was more basic, and the main ingredients were beef, potatoes, chilli and tomatoes. Until today the northern region is well known for the quality of their meat, and a big part of it is exported to other counties.

As well as the love we received from our parents, we inherited the self-confidence you get when you know where you come from and who you are. To this day, they always make sure we don't become distant from our roots.

Having the great advantage of nourishing the traditions of both sides of the country created an amazing symbiosis of flavours in our kitchen.

CARNE ASADA TRADITIONAL
TRADITIONAL MEXICAN BARBECUE

One of my favourite traditions in the north of Mexico is the ritual of the weekend barbecues, "carne asada". It's an all-year-round event.

We always find a good reason to come together. I love the idea of everyone bringing something to it, among friends and family we always identify the ones who make the best guacamole or the best sauces, as you can imagine these tasks are clearly assigned to the best person.

The host is usually responsible for marinating and grilling the beef. Apart from the beef we also like to grill nopales (cactus fruit), corn, spring onions, chillies, cheese, chorizo, vegetables. Of course, no barbecue is complete without a good freshly-made guacamole, refried beans, wheat and corn tortillas, a variety of salsas, and lots of cold beer. We love to end our gathering with good tequila. As we say: "Arriba, abajo, al centro y pa dentro".

BURRITOS DE CARNE ASADA

GRILLED BEEF BURRITOS

approx. 40 m

Serves 4

700 g	beef (flank steak)
8	wheat flour tortillas
100 g	grated Monterey Jack, Gouda or Mozzarella cheese
	salt and pepper
	oil for frying
½	onion (thinly sliced)
1	tomato (cut in half and into thin round slices)
½	iceberg lettuce (cut into thin strips)
1	avocado (sliced)
	mayonnaise
	refried beans (page 126)
	Salsa de Chile de Árbol (page 69)
	Pickled Carrots (page 66)

BURRITOS
are a Mexican dish created in the north of Mexico. Through the years they have been adapted and modified from their original version, specially by Mexican immigrants living in the USA. Burritos are made from wheat flour tortillas.

PREPARATION

If the steak is too thick, cut it in half lengthwise. For this recipe, it is better to use thin slices.
Season the steaks with salt and pepper and fry them in a pan with a little bit of hot oil.
In a pan or comal, gently warm the tortillas on both sides.

TO SERVE

Put the tortillas on a clean surface or plate and spread into the middle lengthwise a teaspoon of mayonnaise, a tablespoon of refried beans, a portion of meat and some cheese, add a few slices of onion, tomato, avocado and iceberg lettuce on top. First fold in the sides at the end of the spread, then roll the burrito with the remaining sides. With a kitchen brush, add some oil on both sides and grill them on a pan until golden brown.

You can serve the burritos with the chile de árbol salsa, the pickled carrots and refried beans.

MY TIP
Before you prepare the burritos, all ingredients should be at hand and ready to use.

Figure
P. 10

HUEVOS RANCHEROS

FRIED EGG AND CORN TORTILLA COVERED IN RED SAUCE

approx. 15 m

Serves 2

4	**eggs**
4	**corn tortillas**
	salsa roja (page 71)
	refried beans (page 126)

Garnish

avocado slices

PREPARATION

Heat the "salsa roja" in a pot with a little bit of hot oil.
(To serve, the salsa and the refried beans must be hot.)

Lightly fry the tortillas in a pan with hot oil. Do not leave the tortillas in the pan too long, otherwise they will be too hard. Then put two deep fried tortillas on a plate and spread over refried beans (1 tablespoon). Fry the eggs (sunny-side up) on the same pan used to fry the tortillas. If necessary, add more oil.

TO SERVE

Place each egg on top of a fried tortilla, and cover them with the hot salsa roja with as much as you like.
You can add avocado slices and refried beans on the side.

Figure
P. 93

BURRITOS DE PAPA
POTATO BURRITOS

Serves 4

approx. 30 m

5	potatoes
3	tomatoes (chopped)
1	garlic clove (peeled and finely chopped)
1	onion (finely chopped)
1	jalapeño chilli (remove stems, seeds and ribs, finely chop)
½ tsp	oregano
	salt and pepper
	oil for frying
4–6	wheat flour tortillas
500 g	refried beans (page 126)
	salsa of your choice

PREPARATION

Peel the potatoes and cut them into small cubes. Heat the water
in a saucepan and boil them (they should not be too soft, they'll be
fried later).
Add a bit of oil on a pan and sauté the onions and garlic. Then add the
chilli and the tomatoes and season with salt, pepper and oregano. Add
the potatoes, reduce the heat and cover the pan, stir once in a while,
continue cooking until they are tender.

TO SERVE

Heat the flour tortillas on both sides. Place the tortilla on a plate. On the centre, spread one tablespoon of refried beans and add 2 table-spoons of potatoes.

First fold in the sides at the end of the spread, then roll the burrito with the remaining sides. Optional: with a kitchen brush, add some oil on both sides and grill them on a pan until golden brown.

"SOL, ARENA Y MAR"
BAJA SEAFOOD

Baja California is a privileged peninsula, bordered on the west by the beautiful deep blue waters of the Pacific Ocean and to the east by the stunning, turquoise waters of the Gulf of California. An area of deserts, fertile valleys and unique plants. The "Desierto de Vizcaino", for example, is a protected biosphere reservoir with huge cactus like the Sahuaro that you can only find in the north of the country.

Fresh seafood enjoys a ubiquitous and prominent place in Baja California's culinary tradition. During my childhood, we spent many vacations on the beaches of San Felipe in the Gulf of California, (196 km from Mexicali) learning to appreciate and love nature and products of the sea.
Among my most vivid memories from those days were our camping holidays in "Punta Estrella", an isolated beach far away from the main town. There was no conventional road to the beach, just lots of sand, beautiful plants and cactus along on the way. The landscape looked like it was from another planet.
I remember the feeling of waking up very early in the morning when it was still a little bit dark, yet you could see the sunlight coming through, hear the sounds of the birds, and smell the ocean, everything was perfect for a great adventure. At this time of the day, the sea water was metres away from the shoreline of the beach, we loved walking through the wet sand looking for shells and mussels. It was also a great opportunity to find octopus. My mother and her friend Esperanza were always in charge of this task, knowing in advance that it would be a matter of luck. My siblings and I were always around "trying to help". I found

it very exciting to be exploring close to the big sea stones, but deep inside I was afraid and I always wished not to be the one to find it.

Every morning, the local fishermen would approach our camping place. They came quietly piloting their modest boats up to the shore. We waited with excitement, sometimes they would let us jump into their boat and, depending on what they caught that day, they sold us shrimp, clams or fish. We spent an incredible week eating and cooking whatever was available from mother nature. Along the Baja California, there are countless small street stalls where seafood is sold, the most famous are shrimp, octopus and clam cocktails, delicious ceviches, seafood tostadas, tacos de pescado and agua chiles, a paradise for seafood lovers. For us, nothing is better after a long night of celebration than starting the next morning with a spicy ceviche or seafood cocktail, the best energy booster!

One of my favourite Baja seafood recipes is "Tacos de Pescado", my crush began many years ago in a small street food stall in Ensenada (240 km from Mexicali), a beautiful city and one of the most important ports in Mexico. This is where the original recipe of "Tacos de Pescado" was created. My mother adapted the original recipe, and to this day, it has remained an important part of our family culinary repertoire.

From one of the most famous street stalls in Ensenada, Anthony Bourdain said:
"Le Bernandin – quality seafood in the street."
No reservations "Baja Episode", 2012

CAMARONES AL MOJO DE AJO
SHRIMP WITH GARLIC AND GUAJILLO CHILLI

Serves 2

approx. 1 h

500 g	fresh shrimp
6	garlic cloves (peeled and thinly sliced)
½	guajillo chilli (remove stems, seeds and ribs)
90 g	butter
1 tsp	lime juice (lemon juice)
2 tbsp	olive oil
	sea salt and pepper

PREPARATION

To peel the shrimp, use your fingers and take the shell and legs off.
With a small knife, carefully remove the digestive track (it is the dark
stripe that runs along the back of the shrimp just beneath the surface).
Using kitchen scissors, cut the guajillo chilli into thin pieces.
In a bowl, mix olive oil, garlic, guajillo chilli, salt and pepper. Add the
shrimp, stir everything and let it rest in the fridge for about 1 hour.
Remove the shrimp from the refrigerator and drizzle with the lime
juice. In a pan with butter, fry the shrimp for about 5 minutes until
they turn pink.

TO SERVE

Serve the shrimp along with rice, green salad and guacamole, or you
can also make delicious tacos with it!

CEVICHE DE PESCADO/ CAMARON

WHITE FISH OR SHRIMP CEVICHE

Figure
P. 99

Serves 4

½ kg	fish (cod, snapper and halibut) or shrimp
1	red onion
2 handfuls	cilantro (finely chopped)
5	limes (juice), if you like you can use more
1–2 tbsp	olive oil
1 pinch	oregano
	sea salt and pepper
	avocado slices
	mayonnaise
	jalapeño chilli (thinly sliced)
6	tostadas (baked corn tortillas)

MY TIP
You could buy the tostadas or make them yourself. When making the tostadas, preheat the oven to 180°C (350 F). Brush the corn tortillas with oil on both sides, place them on a baking sheet and bake for about 5 minutes each side. The result will be crispy golden-brown tortillas.

PREPARATION

Cut the fish into small cubes and put them in to a medium bowl and marinate with the juice of 4 limes, cover with plastic foil and let it rest 1 hour in the fridge.
Halve the onion and cut into thin slices. In a bowl, mix the onion slices and cilantro and marinate with the juice of 1 lime and 1 teaspoon of sea salt and set aside.
Once the fish is ready, add the onion–cilantro mixture, olive oil and mix all the ingredients. Season to taste.

TO SERVE

Take one tostada and spread a teaspoon of mayonnaise, then put 1–2 tablespoons of ceviche on top, add slices of avocado, and you can add jalapeño chilli as an option.
In Mexico, we usually eat ceviche as an appetiser, or with an array of seafood dishes.

TACOS DE SALPICON DE PESCADO – BALTA

TACOS WITH MARINATED SHREDDED FISH

Serves 6

approx. 20 m

12	corn tortillas
6	white fish fillets (cod, snapper, halibut)
3 handfuls	cilantro (finely chopped)
1	bunch (about 10) of radishes (finely chopped)
5	spring onions (chopped)
3 tbsp	olive oil
½	jalapeño chilli (remove stems, seeds and ribs, and finely chop)
2	lime or lemon juice
	sea salt
	pepper
	oregano

PREPARATION

MY TIP
You can also prepare tostadas with it.

Season the fish fillets with salt, pepper and a pinch of oregano. Fry them in a pan with hot oil until golden brown. Put them in a bowl and shred them using a fork.
In a bowl, mix the spring onion, cilantro, radishes and jalapeño chilli with the shredded fish. In a small bowl, combine the olive oil, lime juice, salt and pepper and add to the fish. Mix and season to taste.

TO SERVE

Heat the tortillas in a pan or comal on both sides, place the tortillas in your serving plate and add about 2 tbsp of the fish mixture and serve with guacamole and the salsa of your choice.

SALPICÓN
A preparation of finely chopped ingredients such as vegetables, fish or meat. They are marinated with a vinaigrette and served cold. In Mexico, we serve it on top of tostadas, tortilla chips or corn tortillas.

TACOS DE PESCADO

FISH TACOS

approx. 1,50 h

Serves 4

300 g	white fish (cod, snapper, halibut)
8	corn tortillas
½ cup	flour
½	cabbage (thinly sliced)
	sea salt and pepper
1 pinch	oregano
	oil for frying

For the batter

120 g	wheat flour
1 tsp	salt
1 pinch	oregano
½ tbsp	baking powder
	freshly ground black pepper
80 ml	dark beer
1 tsp	mustard

For the lemon mayonnaise
(as an option, you can add adobo marinated chipotle chilli
for a spicy twist)

3 tbsp	mayonnaise
1 ½ tsp	sour cream or crème fraîche
1 tbsp	lime zest (or lemon peel)
1 tbsp	lime juice (or lemon juice)
2 tbsp	water
	salt

For the pickled onion

1	large onion halved and cut into thin slices
2 tbsp	white wine vinegar
½ tsp	oregano
	sea salt and pepper

Garnish

½	cabbage (thinly sliced)
1	lime quartered
	salsa pico de gallo (page 71)
	avocado slices

Figure
P. 103

PREPARATION

For the fish batter.
Mix the flour, salt, pepper, mustard, oregano and baking powder in a blender and gradually add the beer. The batter should have a creamy texture. When ready, let it rest for 20 minutes in the refrigerator.

MY TIP
While you are waiting for the batter, prepare the salsa pico de gallo, along with the pickled onions and cabbage.

For the mayonnaise
Blend all the ingredients. Season to taste.

For the pickled onion
In a pan with a little bit of oil, sauté the onions until soft, mix continuously (low heat). Put the onions into a bowl and add the vinegar, salt, pepper and oregano, mix everything and set aside for 15 minutes.

Heat the oil in a deep frying pot or wok.
Take the fish batter out of the fridge.
Cut the fish into strips about 10 cm long and 2 cm thick, season with salt and pepper.
Roll the fish fillets in flour and shake off the excess. Then dip the fillets into the batter mixture, drain the excess. Fry the fillets until they are golden brown (be careful not to burn them).

Using kitchen tongs or a skimmer, remove the golden brown fillets and place them over kitchen paper towels to drain the excess oil.

TO SERVE

Heat the tortillas on a pan, cover them with a kitchen towel to keep warm. Set your table with the plate of battered fish, warm tortillas and all the garnish (lemon mayonnaise, pickled onions, cabbage, pico de gallo salsa, avocado slices and any hot sauce of your choice). This is the best way to serve, so everyone can make their own tacos.

How I prepare my tacos: First I spread lemon mayonnaise over the tortilla, then add the fish followed by the salsa pico de gallo, cabbage, pickled onion, avocado slices and a few drops of hot sauce.

LAS FIESTAS

"MÚSICA, FLORES Y TAMALES"
DIA DE MUERTOS

"MUSIC, FLOWERS AND TAMALES"
DAY OF THE DEAD

FESTIVE SEASON

... "The opposite between life and death was not as absolute to the ancient Mexicans as it is to us. Life extended into death, and vice versa. Death was not the natural end of life, but one phase of an infinite cycle. Life, death and resurrection were stages of a cosmic process which repeated themselves continuously ..."
Paz, Octavio. The Labyrinth of Solitude, chapter 3. (1974)

On November 2nd, we celebrate the Day of the Dead, a pre-Hispanic tradition to honour our deceased. Unesco has declared it an Intangible Cultural Heritage of Humanity.

Depending upon where you are from and your family traditions, there are different ways to pay tribute to our loves ones, the persons no longer in this life.

One tradition is going to the cemetery and organising a feast around the deceased's tombstone, decorating it with beautiful flowers (the traditional flower for this day is called cempazúchil), playing their favourite music or singing along with a mariachi band, and in some cases the family will bring food to have a nice meal all together.

Yo lo pregunto

Yo Netzahualcóyotl lo pregunto:
¿Acaso de veras se vive con raíz en la tierra?
Nada es para siempre en la tierra:
Sólo un poco aquí
Aunque sea de jade se quiebra,
Aunque sea de oro se rompe,
Aunque sea plumaje de quetzal se desgarra.
No para siempre en la tierra:
Sólo un poco aquí.

I, Netzahualcoyotl, ask this:
By any chance is it true that one
Lives rooted in the earth?
Not always in the earth:
Here for only just a while;
Though it be made of jade, it breaks;
Though it be made of gold, it breaks;
Though it be made of
quetzal plumage,
It shreds apart.
Not forever here on earth;
Here for only just a while

Nezahualcoyotl, Philosopher and Poet (1402–1472). Translation by John Culr

Another way of celebrating is at home, with a beautiful "altar de muertos". This consists in a wonderful arrangement of flowers, photographs, the deceased's favourite food and drinks mixed with the traditional sweets: calaveritas de azúcar (sugar skulls), alegrías (amaranth bars), pan de muerto (bread of the dead) and colourful Mexican decorations that include papel picado, candles, and different ornaments. It can be as grand as you like it.

During this time, we eat pan de muertos, this is also an important part of this pre-Hispanic tradition, you will find them in every bakery and supermarket around this time. I love it, along with hot chocolate or atole.

Even within all of Mexico, the Day of the Dead is celebrated in different ways, for example in Baja California, where I am from, the tradition of going to the cemetery and singing and eating around the tombstone is rare, but thanks to the migration of people from the south of Mexico (Oaxaca, Michoacán ...) to the north, especially over the past few years, this ancestral tradition is taking on a new meaning.

My parents are not accustomed to celebrating this tradition, we never had an "altar de muertos" at home. The first time I saw one was in Mexico City at my grandmother's house. Her altar was permanent, all year round, she had it in her bedroom, over a small table, full of candles that came in a special glass with the illustration of her beloved saints. Among them you could see the rosaries and scapulars. But on this particular day, she would decorate with flowers and photos of her loved ones.

At the time when I was living in Mexico City in the late 70´s, the idea of the American tradition of Halloween was not popular, barely acknowledged, but that changed drastically in the following years. From those days, I remember the tradition of "La Calaverita". This tradition consisted in going around the neighbourhood on the 1st of November, one day before "dia de muertos". We went door to door singing a funny song asking for candy, and if you where lucky, you would get money. Something very exciting for us was decorating the box where we would receive our candy (mine was a shoe box), the most important ornament was a sugar skull placed in the middle of it and of course being the eldest of my siblings, I was allowed to have a lighted candle as part of my decoration.

La Calavera tiene hambre
no hay un huesito por ahí
no se lo coman todo
déjenos la mitad
La calavera quiere cenar
Cinco de dulce
Cinco de sal.

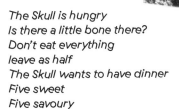

The Skull is hungry
Is there a little bone there?
Don't eat everything
leave as half
The Skull wants to have dinner
Five sweet
Five savoury

Hemispheric Institute, "Pedir Calaverita" (2017)

In the present day, there is renewed awareness and a feeling of honouring our cultural heritage, looking into our past and preserving our traditions. In a Mexico that at times feels lost and broken, we are finding some kind of peace, strength and integrity in our identity as Mexicans.

PAN DE MUERTO – KARLITA

DAY OF THE DEAD BREAD

 approx. 2 h

2 cups	flour
60 ml	warm milk
7.5 g	dry yeast (1 sachet)
100 g	sugar
½ tsp	salt
2	eggs
½ tsp	vanilla extract or the pulp of a vanilla pod
½ tsp	lemon zest or orange zest
4 tbsp	butter (room temperature)
	sugar and melted butter for decoration

PREPARATION

At the time of the arrival of the Spanish in Mexico, the Aztecs where practicing human sacrifice rituals in some ceremonies.
The idea of pan de muerto goes back to this time. It is said that the Spaniards introduced the making of this bread to follow the Aztec tradition of honouring the dead with the main purpose of ending their traditional ceremonies.
The shape and decoration of the bread is full of meanings. The round shape symbolises the cycle of life and death, the cross adorning the top symbolises the bones and the small ball in the middle the skull of the deceased.

This is a recipe from my friend Karla Montfort, who is happy to share it with us.

In a bowl, combine flour, sugar, salt and yeast. Make a hole in the middle of the mixture, crack the eggs in the centre and add the lemon zest, mix everything with a fork. Begin to integrate everything with your hands. Gradually add the milk and butter and keep mixing. Sprinkle a little bit of flour on a clean surface and knead the dough mixture well for 10 minutes. If necessary, add more flour. Put the dough in a bowl, cover with a damp kitchen towel and set aside for 1 ½ hours in a warm place (close to the oven).

Preheat the oven 180°C (350 F).
Put the dough on top of a floured surface. Using a knife, divide it into 6 equal parts. Remove one piece from each one and set aside, we will use this for the bones and skull decoration.
Shape the 6 pieces of dough into round loaves and put them on a greased baking tray. Divide the extra dough into 3 pieces each. With 2 pieces, make a cross and put it on top of the round loaf; with the remaining piece, make a small ball and place it in the centre on top of the cross (bones and skull). Cover it with a clean, damp tea towel and set aside in a warm area for 1 hour and 30 minutes.

Preheat the oven to 180°C (350 F).
Bake the dough for about 15 minutes until it's golden yellow.
To decorate the bread, melt the butter and spread it on top and sprinkle sugar over it.

Figure
P. 109

EL TESORO DE LA FAMILIA
OUR FAMILY TREASURE

This tamales de mole recipe (p. 115) is our culinary jewel. The recipe comes from my abuelita Josefina, who was not really my grandmother, she was my "tía abuela" as we say in Mexico, my abuela Fulvia's sister. She was a great cook and an important figure in our lives. Thanks to my Mother and my aunt Martha, we have kept this recipe alive in our family. This very elaborate but traditional way of preparing tamales de mole is part of our Christmas celebrations. Not many families have this tradition.

Tamales are another great example of the cooking skills of our ancestors.
Already in times of the Aztecs and the Mayas, tamales were a highlight dish on special occasions such as baptisms and weddings.

"Comenzaban a moler el maíz y ponerlo en los paztles ó lebrillos: luego hacian tamales toda la noche y todo el dia por espacio de dos o tres,no dormian de noche sino muy poco trabajando en lo arriba dicho. El dia antes de la boda, convidaban primero a la gente honrada y noble,y despues a la otra gente como eran los maestros de los mancebos.... ."

"They began to grind corn and put it in a clay pot, then they prepared the tamales all day and all night, for two to three days they slept very little at night working on the above. The day before the wedding the gentlemen and noble gentlemen were invited first, then the bachelor's teachers.... ."

Bernardino de Sahagùn, Fray. *Historia Universal de las Cosas de La nueva España Tomo II*, p. 155 (1938)

Our family Christmas season always revolves around the preparation of the tamales de mole. It is hard work for my mother to bring everyone in the family together on this particular date, and although my sister and I live in Europe, we have always somehow managed to be home for these special days. First to arrive is always aunt Martha, full of energy and exotic spices from Chiapas that are normally very hard to find in Mexicali, e.g. chipilin, a plant that they use to make the delicious tamales de chipilin, which we also eat at this time. But really nothing can top our tamales de mole.

The preparation of mole is a pre–Hispanic tradition. The word mole comes from the Nahuatl "mulli" and means something like "mixing". The basic ingredients for a mole are dry chillies and chocolate.

Mole, as it is done today in Mexico, was created in the monasteries after the arrival of the Spaniards. The nuns adapted the original recipe, adding added ingredients from all over the world.

As my sister says, mole is a clear example of fusion cuisine in Mexico, it's an avant–garde dish and stands as a symbol of racial mixing, globalisation, and understanding between cultures.

MÚSICA

PEDRO INFANTE

TAMALES DULCES
SWEET STEAMED CORN MASA PASTRIES

approx. 2 h

15 tamales

15	corn leaves
250 g	corn flour (nixtamalised corn flour)
40 g	amaranth flour (optional)
125 g	butter
½ cup	sugar
300 g	pineapple (canned) finely chopped (keep the juice)
2 tbsp	pineapple juice (canned)
1 tbsp	raisins
1 ½ tsp	baking powder
1–2 cups	milk (room temperature)

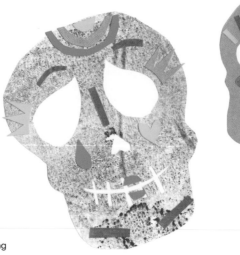
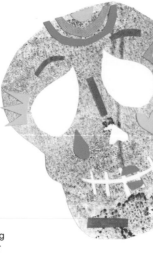

TAMALES
are steamed corn masa
pastries wrapped with a
corn or banana leaf. They
normally come with a filling
and they can be savoury or
sweet. Sweet tamales are
very popular during día de
muertos.

PREPARATION

Soak the corn leaves in a bowl with warm water (15 minutes), remove and dry with a kitchen towel.

For the dough. Using an electric hand mixer, cream the butter in a large bowl. Gradually add the sugar and keep mixing. Add the corn flour, baking powder and mix well by hand. If you have amaranth flour, add this too and mix further. Season the dough and add more sugar if necessary. The dough must be sweeter than normal, as it loses sugar during cooking. Now gradually add the milk. The dough should be mixed for 15 minutes.
At the end, add the pineapple and the pineapple juice to the bowl and mix with your hands.

Take a corn leaf and use a spoon to place 2 tablespoons of the dough into the inside of the leaf in the lower centre. Fold the corn leaf lengthwise first and then crosswise.

To cook the tamales, you need a large steaming pot. Fill the pot with a little bit of water (without covering the steamer plate) and put two coins (pennies) on the bottom of the pot. Insert the steamer plate and place the tamales standing upright next to one another. Make sure no water enters the tamales. Cover the pot with aluminium foil or a kitchen towel and close it with the pot cover. Bring the water to a boil over high heat. When the coins start making noise, it means the water is boiling, now reduce the flame to the lowest heat and continue cooking for an hour.

TO SERVE

These tamales are a delicious dessert, and they can be served warm or at room temperature. Place the tamale on a plate an open it, it is ready to enjoy.

MY TIP
From a corn leaf, using your fingers, you can make thin strips (lengthwise). I like to use them as a cord to close the tamales when they are already folded.

TAMALES DE MOLE – ABUELITA JOSEFINA

MOLE STEAMED CORN MASA PASTRIES

approx. 4 h

25 Tamales

THE BANANA LEAVES

25	**banana leaves**
25	**dry prunes**
25	**almonds (blanched)**
25	**small pieces of fried plantains**
	(cut the plantains in 2 × 2 cm cubes and
	fry briefly in a pan with heated oil)
25	**green olives (pitted)**
25	**thin strips of red pimiento pepper (from a can)**

The banana leaves must be lightly grilled or cooked in water first, to make them softer and smoother to fold later.
Traditionally, the banana leaves are grilled directly over a fire. If you have a gas stove, you can grill them quickly over the flame (be sure not burn them). You will immediately see how their colour and texture changes, they will be softer and easy to fold.
Alternatively, it is also possible to boil water in a large pot and to gradually submerge the leaves into the water, this should also be quick. Afterwards, cut the leaves lengthwise into uniform square sized pieces (about 35 cm long).

THE MEAT

700 g	**chicken (breast or thighs)**
700 g	**pork**
3	**garlic cloves (peeled)**
1	**onion medium**
	salt

Cook the pork with the onion, garlic cloves and salt, approximately 1½ litres of water. After 20 minutes add the chicken. Keep cooking for a total of 40 minutes. Keep the broth, take the meat out, let it cool down and shred with your fingers.

MOLE SAUCE

You can skip the process of making your own mole sauce by using ready-made mole paste, the easiest Mexican brands to find are Mole Doña Maria or Mole La Costeña. The recipe to make mole using a ready-made paste can be found in the recipe for enchiladas de mole (pages 48 – 49).

500 ml	of broth
5	ancho chilli (if you do not find, you can also use mulato chilli)
1	mulato chilli
1	guajillo chilli
1	pasilla chilli
1	jalapeño chilli (dried)
	Clean all the chillies with a kitchen towel and cut them lengthwise. Remove the seeds and ribs.
2 slices	baguette or bread rolls
1	corn tortilla
2	salty crackers
2	butter cookies
2 tbsp	peanuts (unsalted)
2 tbsp	almonds (blanched)
2 tbsp	pecans
2 tbsp	pumpkin seeds
2 tbsp	sesame seeds
3	garlic cloves (peeled)
½	onion (halved)
3	tomatillo verdes (if you cannot find fresh tomatillo, use tomatillos from a tin / drained)
1	large tomato (quartered)
1	mature banana plantain (peeled / sliced)
½	cinnamon stick
3	peppercorns
1 tsp	thyme freshly cut
1 tsp	dried oregano
	salt
100 g	Mexican chocolate (Ibarra) or dark chocolate
5 tsp	lard (for frying)

Figures
P. 114 and P. 158

Before you start preparing the mole, all ingredients should be ready and laid out on your cooking space. All ingredients except chocolate, cinnamon, oregano, thyme, pepper and salt will be lightly fried.

Prepare a medium–sized bowl with a cup of your broth, and set aside.

Heat the lard in a pan or in a fireproof ceramic pot over medium heat. All ingredients are sautéed in it.

Start with the chillies. Sauté them for a very short time and then put them into the bowl with broth. (We start with the chillies, so that they can be softened.)
Then fry the tortilla, slices of bread, crackers and butter biscuits, take them out and bring put them in the bowl. Fry the banana plantain and put them in the bowl, then all the nuts, almonds, pumpkin seeds and repeat the process.
Finally fry the onion with the garlic, tomatoes, tomatillos and sesame seeds and add them into the bowl. While frying, add more lard if needed.

Put the soaking ingredients, along with the broth, into a blender, add thyme, oregano, cinnamon, salt and pepper. Add more broth if needed and mix well. You will need to do this process in two parts, depending on the size of your blender.
Heat 1 teaspoon of lard in a pot and add the mixed ingredients. Add the chocolate together with a little bit of broth (approx. 1 cup) and melt. Try to give the mole a creamy texture. If necessary, add more or less broth. Depending on your taste, you can add more salt, sugar and more chocolate. As a final step, add the meat prepared and stir everything.

THE DOUGH (MASA)

1 kg	corn dough (from about 500 g corn flour and water)
5–7 tbsp	lard
1	peeled and boiled potato
	salt
	a little broth (about ½ cup)

Melt the lard in a large saucepan over a low heat. Mix the dough with the boiled potato and add it together with a bit of broth and heat at low flame, stirring constantly. Taste and add salt. Make sure that the dough does not burn. Add more lard where needed. The dough should be smooth, soft and creamy and a bit salty, as it loses salt during cooking.

TAMALES ENSEMBLE

Put all ingredients in small bowls. Then place a prepared banana leaf on the worktop. Spread 3–4 tablespoons of dough, press it a bit flat and add 2–3 tbs of the mole preparation. Place a dried plum, an olive, a piece of the plantain, a strip of red pimiento pepper and an almond on top. Then fold the banana leaf into a packet and set aside.

To cook the tamales, you need a large steaming pot. Fill the pot with a little bit of water (without covering the steamer plate) and put two coins (pennies will be good) on the bottom of the pot. Insert the steamer plate and place the tamales standing upright next to one another. Make sure no water enters the tamales. Cover the pot with aluminium foil or a kitchen towel and close it with the pot cover. Bring the water to a boil over high heat. When the coins start making noise, it means the water is boiling, now reduce the flame to the lowest heat and continue cooking for an hour.

TO SERVE

The tamales are served warm and unfolded directly on the plate. They are usually served together with verduritas curtidas (pickled vegetables – page 13☉) and aderezo de champiñones (mushroom vinaigrette, page 133).

MY TIP
The tamales that are left or not going to be eaten can be frozen and warmed later in the microwave.

118

ATOLE DE NUEZ
HOT DRINK WITH WALNUTS

approx 15 m

Serves 4

1 L	milk
5 tbsp	sugar
1 cup	walnuts or pecan nuts
	(you can also use strawberries or vanilla extract)
5 tsp	cornstarch
¼ cup	cold water
1 tsp	cinnamon or a cinnamon stick

PREPARATION

Dissolve the cornstarch with the cold water and set aside. In a blender, grind the walnuts with 1 cup of milk. In a saucepan, bring the rest of the milk to boil and add the ground walnuts and cinnamon. Reduce the heat and gradually add the cornstarch. Then add the sugar and keep cooking and stirring over low heat until it thickens.

ATOLE
is one of the most traditional Mexican hot drinks, we serve it with breakfast or before dinner. At home, we mostly drink atole in winter, during the Christmas season and during the Dia de los Muertos. Our favourites are atole with vanilla, strawberries or walnuts.

This delicious drink comes from the era of the Aztecs. The original recipe consisted of corn dough dissolved in hot water, and they would add different types of chilli, honey or cacao.

LA CALAVERA

9

FAVORITO

★ ★ ★ ★ ★

II. VAMOS A ECHARNOS UNOS TACOS

→	A LA PARRILLA	70
→	A LA PLANCHA	80
→	AL PASTOR	90
→	DE BARBACOA	100
→	DE BIRRIA	112
→	DE CABEZA	122
→	DE CANASTA	132
→	DE CARNITAS	142
→	DE CHILORIO	154

CLOSEST TO MY HEART

These are the recipes that remind me of the joyful moments of cooking with my mother.
Some are main dishes, whereas others are perfect side dishes for many of the recipes in the book.

COCHINITA PIBIL
BAKED PORK WITH ACHIOTE

approx. 7 h

Serves 8

1 kg	**pork shoulder or loin (you can also use chicken)**
500 g	**pork ribs**
	sea salt and pepper

for the marinade sauce

80 g	**achiote paste**
1 cup	**orange juice**
¼ cup	**lime juice**
1 tbsp	**vinegar (white wine or apple cider vinegar)**
4	**garlic cloves (peeled)**
¼	**large onion**
½ tsp	**cinnamon**
1 tsp	**sea salt**
½ tsp	**oregano**
1	**spice clove**
½ tsp	**cumin**
5	**black peppercorns**
	lard or oil (for frying)
4	**large banana leaves for cooking**
	(can be found in Asian supermarkets)

This is one of the most famous dishes of the Yucatan Peninsula. "Pibil" is an ancient Mayan cooking technique in which a hole is first dug in the ground. Then a fire is lit in the hole, covered with stones, and the food is then wrapped in banana leaves. In the end, everything is covered with earth. The result was a delicious slow-roasted meat. In Yucatan they still prepare it in this traditional way.

The following recipe shows how Cochinita Pibil is prepared in my mother's kitchen.

To Serve
Salsa de chile habanero con cebolla morada (page 64)
Frijoles negros refritos (refried beans) (page 126)
Arroz con cilantro (rice with cilantro) (page 124)
Guacamole (page 37)

PREPARATION

Cut the meat into medium-sized pieces (it is easier to marinate and they will cook faster), season with salt and pepper. In a blender, mix all the ingredients for the marinade sauce. Let it marinate for at least 3 hours. It is even better if you let it marinate in the fridge overnight.

Preheat the oven to 160°C (320 F).

Figure
P. 3

Clean the banana leaves with a damp cloth and cover the bottom of your oven pot or casserole dish with 4 leaves, laid crosswise. The leaves are later folded together and must cover the entire meat. Spread the marinated meat over with all the sauce, I like to add ½ cup of drinking water. Fold the banana leaves together, they must cover the meat. Sprinkle some water onto the banana leaves, so they will not dry. Cover the pot with aluminium foil, put a lid on it and bake co-chinita pibil for about 3 hours. After 2 hours, check how far the meat is cooked. If it's too dry, you can add more water. The meat must be tender at the end.

MY TIP
Traditionally, the meat is covered with banana leaves and baked in the oven. But you can do it without the leaves and also cook it using a slow cooker or a pot over the stove.

TO SERVE

Cochinita pibil is served with arroz con cilantro (rice with cilantro), frijoles negros refritos (refried beans), guacamole and salsa de chile habanero with cebolla morada. (Habanero and red onion sauce). I highly recommend making tacos with cochinita pibil!

ARROZ CON CILANTRO
RICE WITH CILANTRO

approx. 20 m

Serves 4

2 cups	rice
1 handful	fresh cilantro (chopped)
1 small can	corn (discard liquid)
½	onion cut into small cubes
4 cups	water
2 tsp	oil
1 tsp	salt or chicken broth

PREPARATION

In a blender, mix the cilantro with salt, garlic and 4 cups of water. In a saucepan with hot oil, sauté the onion, add the rice and keep frying until the rice changes colour, don't burn. Then add the water–cilantro mixture and the corn, bring to a boil, reduce the heat, cover and continue to simmer for about 10 minutes on low heat.

COCHITO — TIA MARTHA

BAKED PORK RIBS

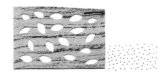

 approx. 7 h

Serves 4

1 kg	**pork ribs**
3	**dry pasilla chillies**
3	**dry ancho chillies**
1 cup	**water from the cooked chillies**
¼	**onion**
3	**cloves garlic (peeled)**
1 sprig	**fresh thyme**
½ tsp	**oregano**
½ tsp	**black peppercorns**
¼ cup	**vinegar (apple cider vinegar or white wine vinegar)**
½ tsp	**cinnamon**
	sea salt

COCHITO
is a pork dish specialty
from Chiapas and one
of my dad's favourite
dishes. It is part of the
gastronomical identity of
region and a very popular
dish during the january
holiday season (fiestas) in
the province of Chiapa de
Corzo. The original recipe
uses different parts of the
pork.

MY TIP
The marinated meat can
also be cooked in a pot
on the stove or in a slow
cooker.

PREPARATION

With kitchen scissors cut the chilli peppers lengthwise, remove stem, seeds and ribs. Boil water in a pot and turn off the heat. Add the dry chilli peppers and leave them in the water until they are soft. Take them out and keep 1 cup of water and set aside.

Prepare the marinade by blending all ingredients together with a cup of chilli water. Then marinate the meat with the sauce and let it rest in the refrigerator for at least 4 hours, preferably the whole night.

Preheat the oven to 160°C (320 F). Put the meat with the remaining marinade in a fireproof dish with a lid and bake for about 1 hour.

TO SERVE

Serve the cochito with rice, frijoles negros refritos (refried beans) (page 126), ensalada de repollo verde con aguacate (page 132) and salsa de chile habanero con cebolla morada (page 64).

FRIJOLES NEGROS REFRITOS

BLACK OR PINTO REFRIED BEANS

approx. 2 h

Serves 6

4 cups	cooked black beans
½ cup	beans cooking water
½	onion
½ tsp	dried oregano
2	cloves garlic (peeled)
1 piece	mild chorizo (optional)
	salt
	oil for frying

PREPARATION

Put the beans in a large pot, cover with water and bring to a boil together with the garlic cloves, onion and oregano. Reduce the heat, cover and cook for about 1 ½ hours. When the beans are tender, add the salt and season to taste.

Using a blender, lightly mash the beans with half a cup of the bean cooking water (if pieces of cooked onion or garlic get into the blender, that's ok, as they provide more flavour). It must have a thick consistency. If necessary, add more bean water.
Cut the chorizo in to small pieces and fry them in a pan with a little bit of oil, add the mashed beans and sauté briefly over low heat. Taste and add more salt as needed.

MY TIP
It is easier to cook the beans if they have been soaked in water the night before. Drain the water before cooking, and add new water. You can use an express pressure cooker to save lots of time. You can also skip this step if you buy the beans already cooked (canned beans).

ENSALADA DE FRIJOLES NEGROS

BLACK BEAN SALAD

approx. 2 h

Serves 4

2–3 cups	**cooked beans (drained)**
1	**large tomato cut into small cubes**
½	**onion (finely chopped)**
1 handful	**fresh cilantro (finely chopped)**
1 pinch	**oregano**
2 tbsp	**olive oil**
1 tbsp	**apple cider vinegar**
	salt and pepper

PREPARATION

MY TIP
You can also use canned beans, e.g. "La Costeña" or "La Sierra".

Mix 2 cups of cooked beans with the onion, tomatoes, cilantro, olive oil and vinegar. Mix everything and season with oregano, salt and pepper.

SOPA DE FRIJOL NEGRO

BLACK BEAN SOUP

 approx. 2 h

Serves 6

500 g	**black beans**
½	**onion**
2	**garlic cloves (peeled)**
½ tsp	**dried "epazote" or oregano**
3	**medium-sized tomatoes**
½	**jalapeño chilli (stem, seeds and ribs removed)**
3–4 cups	**water from cooked beans**
1 tsp	**sea salt**
	oil for frying

To serve

4	**corn tortillas**
50 g	**feta cheese (Mexican fresco or Cotija cheese)**
1	**avocado**

PREPARATION

Place the beans in a large pot, cover with water and bring them to boil together with 1 clove of garlic, ¼ onion and dried epazote or oregano. Reduce the heat, cover the pot and cook for about 1 hour. When the beans are tender, add the salt and season to taste. Remove 3–4 cups of the bean water and set aside.
Purée the boiled beans with 2 cups of the bean water in a blender.
Fry the rest of the ingredients in a pan without oil. Remove the ingredients from the pan and blend. Fry this sauce in a pan with oil and add the bean puree, stir and cook for another 5 minutes. The *sopa de frijol* should not be too thick. If necessary, add more bean water. Stir everything, let it cook a little more and season to taste.

Cut the corn tortillas into small squares, fry the tortilla pieces in a deep pan with hot oil, remove and drain on kitchen paper.

TO SERVE

Place a portion of the bean soup in a bowl, add a few pieces of tortilla chips, sprinkle with cheese and decorate with a slice of avocado.
You could also add a tablespoon of sour cream.

MY TIP
It's easier to cook the beans if you let them soak in water the night before. Drain before cooking.

Figure
P. 129

TODOS QUEREMOS

VERDURITAS CURTIDAS

PICKLED VEGETABLES

approx. 1 day

3	carrots cut into small cubes
1	zucchini cut into small cubes
2	spring onions (or normal onions) finely chopped
6	jalapeño chillies (remove the stem) cut into thin slices
6	garlic cloves (peeled)
1 tbsp	oregano
1	bay leaf
2	sprigs of thyme
2 tbsp	sea salt
6	black peppercorns
1–2 cups	apple cider vinegar or white wine vinegar
	glass jar with a lid

PREPARATION

MY TIP
This a perfect side dish for tamales de mole or to go along with meat.

Distribute the jalapeño chillies on the bottom of the jar. Place the garlic cloves on top and make layers with the rest of the ingredients. Add the salt and peppercorns and carefully pour in the vinegar until all ingredients are covered 1 cm above the last layer. Close the jar and leave to marinate for at least 1 day.

CALABaCiTA

ENSALADA DE NOPALES

CACTUS SALAD

Serves 4

500g	**cooked cactus strips**
	(if you can't find them fresh you can use store bought nopales, they come with a vinegar marinade. In this case don't add more vinegar)
½	**onion (finely chopped)**
2 tbsp	**grated cheese (Feta cheese or Mexican Añejo cheese)**
1	**tomato cut into small cubes without seeds**
1 handful	**fresh cilantro (finely chopped)**
2 tbsp	**olive oil**
1 tbsp	**white vinegar**
	sea salt

approx. 10 m

PREPARATION

When using fresh nopales, cut them in to cubes, put them in a bowl and add 2 tbsp of coarse salt. Let them rest, they will release a sticky substance and normally will foam. Once cooked, drain and rinse the nopales. On a pan, with a little bit of oil, cook the nopales until they are tender. Let them cool down, put them in a bowl and add the tomatoes, onion, the olive oil, vinegar and cilantro. Season to taste and sprinkle the cheese on top.

Using already cooked nopales:
Remove the nopales from the glass jar, drain and rinse briefly.
Cut the nopales into cubes and place in a bowl.
Add the tomato, onion, cilantro, olive oil and salt and stir well.

TO SERVE

Sprinkle the salad with the cheese.

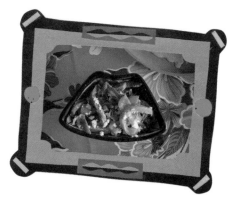

ENSALADA DE REPOLLO VERDE CON AGUACATE

WHITE CABBAGE AND AVOCADO SALAD

approx. 10 m

Serves 6

½	white cabbage
1	avocado
3 tbsp	olive oil
1 ½ tbsp	lime or lemon juice
1 handful	cilantro (finely chopped)
1 tsp	oregano
	sea salt and pepper

PREPARATION

Slice the cabbage into thin strips, placing the strips in a medium bowl. In a small bowl, stir in the olive oil, lime juice, cilantro, oregano, salt and pepper. Add the mix to the cabbage.
Before serving, halve the avocado, removing the seed, cut into cubes and mix with the cabbage.

ADEREZO DE CHAMPIÑONES

MUSHROOM VINAIGRETTE

approx. 1,5 h

500 g	mushrooms
15	black peppercorns
5	garlic cloves (peeled)
5 tbsp	Worcestershire sauce
2 ½ tbsp	mustard
15 tbsp	white wine vinegar
1 cup	olive oil
2 ½ tbsp	spring onions (finely chopped)
2 ½ tbsp	parsley
2 ½ tbsp	lemon juice
1 tsp	sea salt

PREPARATION

In a mortar (molcajete), crush the salt, pepper and garlic, then put it in a bowl. Add the vinegar, olive oil, the mustard and mix everything. Cover the bowl and let it rest for about 30 minutes (not in the fridge). About 1 hour before serving, cut the mushrooms into thick slices, place in a bowl and mix with the marinade.
Just before serving, add the lemon juice, spring onions and parsley to the mushrooms and mix everything.

TO SERVE

Place the mushroom vinaigrette on romaine lettuce leaves. A perfect side dish for tamales de mole, Christmas turkey or any meat.

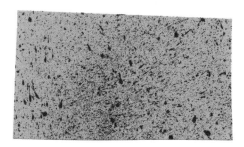

POLLO EN SALSA DE CHILE CHIPOTLE

CHIPOTLE SAUCE CHICKEN

 approx. 30 m

Serves 4

4	chicken breast fillets
1 – 2	chillies "Chipotle en Adobo" from a can
1 ½ cups	sour cream
½	onion
100 g	mushrooms
30 g	butter
	salt and pepper
1 tbsp	oil for frying

PREPARATION

Simple, fast and delicious!!! I love the smoky taste of chipotle chillies.

Cut the chicken breast fillets in half and season with salt and pepper. Cut the onion and the mushrooms into thin slices. Blend the sour cream and the chipotle chillies together with salt and pepper. In a pan with butter and oil, sauté the onions and mushrooms and add the chipotle cream. In another pan with oil, fry the chicken breast fillets from both sides.

TO SERVE

Place a portion of the chicken on a serving plate and add the chipotle cream over the chicken. Serve with rice.

Figures
P. 134 and P. 157

"DULCES TENTACIONES"

SWEET TEMPTATIONS

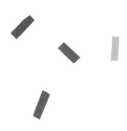

Many of the Mexican traditional desserts were developed when the Spaniards settled in Mexico and established their first monasteries. The recipes were inspired by European cuisine and adapted with local fruits and ingredients.

When I started travelling, I discovered that many of my favourite traditional Mexican desserts, such as rice pudding, where not original Mexican creations!

Sugar was first introduced in Mexico by the Spanish conquerors. Before this, the Mayans and Aztecs sweetened their food and drinks with honey and agave syrup. Honey had a special place in the heart of the Mayan culture.

They were beekeepers. The Mayans used it for ceremonies as well as for medical treatments. They are still known for their wide knowledge of honey bee production and bees' ecosystem circle. The Maya region is still one of the biggest producers of honey in Mexico. In the Yucatán Peninsula there are bees that are indigenous to the region.

Preparing desserts at home is still a big tradition in Mexico, and the recipes are handed down from generation to generation. One of them is Flan. A perfect dessert and one of my favourites – easy to make and always highly praised by friends and family.

ALEGRIAS

AMARANTH BARS

◀ approx. 45 m

ALEGRIAS
are among the most
popular sweets in Mexico.
We find them everywhere
and in many forms.
The main ingredient is
amaranth, in Nahuatl,
it is called "huautli".
For the Mayas and Aztecs,
amaranth was an important
source of nutrition. They
also used the seeds
in special ceremonies.
The Aztec women used
amaranth seeds and honey
to make figures in honour
of the god Huitzilopochtli.

... *"El amaranto, que servía
para elaborar las esculturas
comibles, subió por los
cielos, lo mismo que las
plumas de colibrír que se
utilizaban para decorarlo."*

*"The amaranth, used to
make the edible sculptures,
rose into the sky, as did
the hummingbird feathers
used for decoration."*
Esquivel, Laura. *Malinche*,
p. 154. (2008)

The Spanish conquerors
recognised the importance
of amaranth as part of
Aztec religious rituals. It is
said that for this reason,
after the arrival of the
Spanish, the production
of amaranth radically
collapsed.

for 10–15 bars

200 g	puffed amaranth
5 tbsp	pecan nuts (or walnuts)
5 tbsp	dried cranberries
5 tbsp	pumpkin seeds
1 cup	honey
1 cup	brown sugar or piloncillo (Mexican pure brown sugar)
	a few drops of lemon juice

PREPARATION

In a pan without oil, briefly roast the amaranth, pumpkin seeds and pecans (do not burn), remove and put them into a medium bowl and mix.

In a sauce pan, caramelise the sugar, add the honey and lemon drops and keep cooking over a low heat, stirring constantly, until everything is liquid.

Carefully pour the caramel into the bowl with the roasted ingredients, mix everything with a wooden spoon.

Cover a baking sheet or ceramic baking dish with baking paper, spread the amaranth mixture with a spoon over the baking paper, cover with another layer of baking paper and press down with your hands to flat surface. Let everything rest and after about 35 minutes, remove the upper baking paper and with a knife, cut the alegrias into rectangular pieces (as big as you like them)

FLAN
CREAMY CUSTARD DESSERT

approx. 1 h

Serves 8

5	**eggs**
1 can	**sweetened condensed milk**
1 can	**evaporated milk**
1 cup	**milk**
1 tbsp	**vanilla extract**
200 g	**brown sugar**

PREPARATION

preheat the oven to 180°C (350 F)

In a pan on low heat, slowly caramelised the sugar until it becomes liquid (continuously stirring). Quickly pour the caramel into a baking pan and move it around so the caramel swirls around on the inside (covering the bottom and walls). Allow it to cool down.
In a blender, mix the rest of the ingredients. Pour the mixture into the baking pan and cover it with aluminium foil (be sure it is well covered). Place the baking pan (with the mixture) into the middle of a large and deep oven tray or baking dish. Pour in hot water until you reach half of the baking pan and then carefully place it into the oven (This baking process is called a "water bath").
Bake the flan for 45 minutes.

Remove the baking dish from the oven and carefully take the baking pan out of the hot water. Let it cool to room temperature, then place in the refrigerator for a minimum or 1 hour.

TO SERVE

Flan its best served cold. When it is ready to serve, invert the baking pan onto a serving plate, allowing the flan to drop out and the caramel sauce to flow over it.

PASTEL DE ELOTE – TIA MARTHA

CORN CAKE

approx. 1 h

350 g	corn kernels (canned)
5	eggs
150 g	flour
1 tbsp	baking powder
90 g	butter (room temperature)
1 can	evaporated milk
1 can	sweetened condensed milk
1 tsp	cinnamon powder
1 tsp	vanilla extract or the inside of a vanilla pod
1 pinch	salt
	extra butter and flour for the baking pan

PREPARATION

preheat the oven to 180°C (350 F)

In a blender, mix the different types of milk, corn, vanilla and cinnamon. In large bowl, using an electric mixer, cream the butter and add the eggs one by one, continue with the flour and baking powder and mix until integrated. Finally, add the milk mixture and mix.

Grease a round (26 cm) or square baking pan and sprinkle with flour and cover with baking paper. Then pour the prepared mix and bake everything for about 45 minutes.

You can test whether the cake is done by inserting a toothpick, it has to come out clean.

Figures
P. 4 and P. 143

PLATANO FRITO
FRIED PLANTAINS

approx. 10 m

Serves 2

2	plantains
1 tbsp	brown sugar (or agave syrup)
½ tsp	cinnamon
60 g	butter
1 tsp	oil for frying
	sour cream or crème fraîche
	vanilla ice cream (optional)

PLATANOS FRITOS
are our favourite dessert during Christmas season. There are different ways to enjoy them, this is the way we prepare them at home.

The plantains must be ripe, you will be able to tell they are ready because their colour is a mixture of yellow and black. You will find them at Asian or Latin American supermarkets. Sometimes you will find them unripe, green coloured; if this is the case, you can follow the same procedure as with the avocados. I leave them in the oven, wrapped in newspaper from 2–4 days before using them.

PREPARATION

Peel and halve the plantains. Then cut the halves again horizontally, lengthwise. In a pan, melt the butter together with the oil on medium heat. Fry the pieces on both sides until golden brown.

TO SERVE

Place the fried plantain pieces on a plate and spread some brown sugar, sour cream and cinnamon powder on top. Optionally serve with a scoop of vanilla ice cream.

Figure
P. 145

144

UNESCO has declared Traditional Mexican Cuisine as an "Intangible Cultural Heritage of Humanity" *

*UNESCO, 2010

Thank you, Anne, for this fantastic journey, for your creative vision and love of Mexico.

Thank you "mi amor", Lars Wenkel, for your patience, your incredible photos and unconditional support.

Thank you, Andreas Kannengießer, for your amazing photos, commitment and always giving your best energy to make this book possible.

To my siblings, Karen, Omar and Ivan, to my sisters- and brothers-in-law Araceli, Gisel, Jens and Ian, to my in-laws, Heide and Kal-Otto Wenkel, thank you for your support and always being there.

To my best friend, Karla Montfort, I am grateful for your friendship and for sharing with me your knowledge and experience in the cooking world.

Ivette Pérez de Wenkel

Thank you, my dear Z.
You are the best supporter, funniest consultant and most loving partner in crime
I could wish for.

Anne Wenkel

Achiote paste (Pasta de Achiote / Nahuatl achiotl)
The Achiote plant is a shrub from whose seeds the heart-shaped capsule fruit achiote paste is made. This paste gives the dishes a special taste and the typical red colour. Especially common on the Yucatan Peninsula.

Agave Syrup (Miel de Agave)
Agave syrup is a sweetener made from a special kind of agave plant. In Mexico, before the Spaniards arrived, and depending on the region, there were many different names for this plant. The Spaniards called this plant "Maguey". In 1753, a Swedish scientist toured the area and stated that the scientific name for this plant should be "agave". Our famous tequila is made from the blue agave.

Amaranth (Amaranto)
Amaranth is a pseudo-grain, whose grains contain a wealth of easily-digestible nutrients, high-quality proteins and valuable minerals such as iron, calcium and magnesium. It is a food that is perfect for people with gluten intolerance.

Comal
The comal is one of the most important kitchen tools in Mexico. It was originally made of clay and shaped into a disk. Today, they are made of sheet metal, iron steel and have different shapes. The Mexicans used the comal to make their tortillas long before the Spaniards arrived. It's used also to toast or sauté grains and chillies, and to warm up food.

Chile de Árbol
Fresh or dried, chile de árbol is very spicy. It grows green on the bush and changes colour from green to red when ripe. Dried is the most common way to use it.

Chilli Ancho
It's a dried poblano chilli that has an intense dark red colour after drying.

Chilli Chipotle
It's a dried jalapeño chilli whose colour changes from green to dark red or blackish brown when dried. Drying also changes the taste and makes it more intense.

Chilli Chipotle en Adobo
It's a dried jalapeño chilli that has been marinated in a smoky sauce. You can usually find it canned. It's flavour is mild.

Chilli Guajillo
It's a dried chilli of the mirasol chilli variety. It is medium hot.

Chilli Habanero
Originating from the Amazon rainforest in South America, it is one of the hottest chillies in the world. It grows green on the tree and changes colour from green to red-orange or when ripe.

Chilli Jalapeño
It's a medium-sized green chilli and one of the most famous chillies of Mexico. It is used fresh or pickled.

Chilli Morita
It's a chilli that is obtained by drying small jalapeño chillies. It's spicier than the chipotle chilli.

Chilli Mulato
Like chilli ancho, it's a poblano chilli that has a dark brown colour after drying. The taste is a little sweet.

Chilli Pasilla
It's a dried chilaca chilli. It's mild and has a bitter chocolate aroma.

Chilli Piquin or Chilli Chiltepin
It's a small round dried red chilli. Very spicy.

Epazote
It's an aromatic herb, known in Europe as Jesuit tea or Mexican gland geese foot. Epazote is an ancient Aztec spice plant. In Mexico we use it in various dishes as a seasoning herb. e.g. for cooked beans.

Hibiscus flowers (Flor de Jamaica)
Hibiscus is a plant of the mallow family, which is native to Africa and tropical regions of Asia. In Mexico, the dried flowers are used for fresh drinks or for vegetarian dishes. The flowers have an intense red colour and a sour taste.

Rice Water (Agua de Horchata)
It's a cold drink of Arab origin which was introduced by the Spaniards to Mexico. In Mexico, it is made with rice, milk, water, vanilla, cinnamon and sugar.

Huitzilopochtli
Was the Aztec god of war and the sun. The name means "hummingbird, the left side or hummingbird of the south" and has its origin in the Aztec belief that upon dying, every warrior embodies a hummingbird. According to Aztec beliefs, the left side meant the south, the direction in which the dead went.

Coriander (Cilantro)
is an aromatic herb originating in North Africa and Asia.

Molcajete
(Mortar)

It's the symbol of Mexican gastronomic culture and a mortar made of volcanic rock, mainly used for mashing tomatoes, spices, chilli peppers, onions, garlic, etc.

Náhuatl

Was the most important language during the Aztec empire. Today, it remains the most important indigenous language in Mexico, and more than one million Mexicans speak it daily.

Nopales
(Cactus)

It's a cactus plant that has been a food for us Mexicans for thousands of years. Nopales appears as a symbol in the centre of our national coat of arms along with the royal eagle and the serpent, which are decorated with an oak branch and an olive branch.

Oregano
(Lippia graveloens)

is an aromatic spice of Mediterranean origin. There are different varieties, but one of the most important ones used in gastronomy is cultivated in Mexico.

Tortilla Press
(Prensa para Tortillas)

It's a very practical tool used to make tortillas. Originally, the tortillas were formed by hand. Tortilla presses are usually made of wood or iron.

Tostadas

Are crispy corn tortillas. They are made by frying, baking or grilling the tortillas.

Tomatillo verde
(Physalis ixocarpa)

is a plant that is indigenous to Mexico. The fruit of the Tomatillo Verde is small, spherical, slightly flattened, green and surrounded by a paper-like shell. The taste is more acidic than red tomatoes.

Vanilla
(Vainilla)

It's a Mexican aromatic plant of the orchid variety. After the vanilla pods have been fermented, the vanilla is extracted.

Difficulty

Easy

Medium

Complex

Time

Spiciness

Mild

Medium

Hot

Very hot

Vegetarian

= LA COCINERA =

151

ANNE WENKEL ～ ILLUSTRATION

Anne Wenkel is a freelance Illustrator and artist born in 1983 in former East Germany. Her drawing career started when she was about 4 years old — and since then crayons have been her best friend. She loves to experiment with analogue techniques and mixing different media. This includes woodcuts, ink drawings and paper cuts, combined with bits of digital elements and hand-lettering.

The biggest influence on her work is her love of travelling and discovering the world with all its inspiring cultures and visual impacts that can be found on every corner. In 2014, she welcomed her son Oskar into the world, in 2017, her son Wim followed. She lives in Berlin together with her partner, director and filmmaker Andreas Kannengießer, and the kids.

IVETTE PÉREZ DE WENKEL ～ TEXT

Ivette Pérez de Wenkel (neé Pérez Arteche) was born in Mexico City in 1969. She studied Communication Sciences at Universidad Iberoamericana in Tijuana, Baja California. After 9 years working in the advertising world as a copywriter and project manager, she decided to move to London where she worked at the Mexican Embassy.

In 2013, she moved to Berlin and began pursuing her passion of food and cooking. And within just a few years, she has evolved in the world of gastronomy as a caterer, cooking teacher and author of cookbooks.

Pollo en Salsa Chipotle
P. 135

COD:157

CHILE CHIPOTLE

$120.00 KG

Tortilla de Maíz
PP. 46 – 47

Tacos de Pollo al Pastor
PP. 78 – 79

Salsa de Chile Habanero
con Cebolla morada
P. 64

IMPRINT

ISBN: 978-1-58423-734-1

English Edition published in 2019 by

GINGKO PRESS

Gingko Press Inc.
2332 Fourth Street, Suite E
Berkeley, CA 94710, USA
Phone: +1 (510) 898-1195
books@gingkopress.com
gingkopress.com

Gingko Press Verlags GmbH
Schulterblatt 58
D-20357 Hamburg, Germany
Phone: +49 (0)40-291425
gingkopress@t-online.de

English Edition © Gingko Press Inc. 2019
German Edition published in 2017 by Jaja Verlag, Berlin

Texts:
Ivette Pérez de Wenkel

Illustrations:
Anne Wenkel (annewenkel.com)

Photographs:
Andreas Kannengießer (andreaskannengiesser.de),
Lars Wenkel (larswenkel.com)

Layout Concept:
Raby-Florence Fofana

Layout & Typesetting for the English Edition:
Weiß-Freiburg GmbH Graphik & Buchgestaltung

Copyediting for the English Edition:
John Stilwell

Editorial Managment for the English Edition:
Anika Heusermann

Fonts:
Grilly Type
GT Haptik — Regular, Regular Rotalic,
Regular Oblique, Light, Bold, Bold Rotalic
grillitype.com

Printed in China